SPIRITUAL
RESISTANCE
AGENT FIELD
MANUAL

HOW TO BE A FORCE FOR GOOD IN ENEMY TERRITORY

WHAT OTHERS ARE SAYING
ABOUT THIS BOOK . . .

"With conflicts rising all around us, the time has never been more important to bravely take a stand and, by that stand, not only change ourselves but inspire change in others. No matter the circumference of our circle of influence—large or small—we can make a difference. That is the message Kathryn Lee Moss so beautifully delivers in her book, *Spiritual Resistance Agent Field Manual*. If small helms turn large ships, this book, with its succinct portraits of courage, is such a helm. Beautifully and passionately written with a high degree of personal transparency, I was left with this lasting realization: in resisting evil, we are not alone, and we never will be. History is replete with pioneers who have, in their respective stances, paved the way for all those who follow to likewise be a force for good in enemy territory."

—William A. Donne (author of *We Will End the Conflict Now*)

"In her inspired book, *Spiritual Resistance Agent Field Manual*, author Kathryn Moss does one of the many things she does so well: tell inspirational stories. As a playwright and speaker, Kathyrn has engaged multiple audiences with her clear and intriguing tales of those who have fought for good in the face of evil. She waves her magic wand again in this timely, captivating, and often personal read. I am so darn excited to share this book with my children and my young grandchildren. The evil around us can be successfully fought with spiritual resistance. This book is a fantastic guide!"

—Mary Joanne Bell (author of *The Pursuit of Happi-nest*)

SPIRITUAL
RESISTANCE
AGENT FIELD
MANUAL

HOW TO BE A FORCE FOR
GOOD IN ENEMY TERRITORY

KATHRYN LEE MOSS

CFI
An imprint of Cedar Fort, Inc.
Springville, Utah

Bible verses included in the text of this book are from the King James Version of the Bible except where otherwise noted.

ISBN 13: 978-1-4621-4295-8

Published by CFI, an imprint of Cedar Fort, Inc.
2373 W. 700 S., Springville, UT 84663
Distributed by Cedar Fort, Inc., www.cedarfort.com

Library of Congress Control Number: 2022935662

Cover design by Courtney Proby
Cover design © 2022 Cedar Fort, Inc.
Edited and typeset by Spencer Skeen

Printed in the United States of America

10 9 8 7 6 5 4 3 2 1

Printed on acid-free paper

To my dearest family.
Thank you for being part of my penguin huddle.

A NOTE ON USING THIS MANUAL

This training manual is designed after the Special Operations Executive training manual from World War II, which was used to train resistance agents in Britain. Each chapter contains three sections to illustrate the principle being taught: a personal story, a Bible story and a story from history. Each section also contains questions to talk or journal about and ideas for individuals and families to try. It can be used as a reference manual and does not need to be read in order.

"The aim of this training is to present a clear picture of the forces which oppose them. By this means the agent is able to understand the nature of the opposition, the degree of danger to be expected, and will have a basis for planning measures of self protection."

—Special Operations Executive Manual

CONTENTS

SECTION 4:

INTRODUCTION

RESISTANCE MOVEMENT (ri-ˈzi-stən(t)s ˈmuːvmənt) *noun*.
An organized effort by a portion of the general population to withstand an invader or occupying power.

The word "resist" means to fight against or refuse to give into something. When the Nazis invaded most of Europe during World War II, each country's government ended up surrendering, but there were regular citizens in each and every occupied country who stood together to fight against the occupation of their homeland. Resistance movements sprang up in France, Belgium, Poland, Norway, and even in Germany itself!

These were people who recognized the evil of their day and steadfastly refused to follow it. There were many different kinds of resistance fighters and many, many different ways that they resisted. But they all did whatever they could and sacrificed whatever was necessary to resist the evil, hatred, and lies they saw around them.

On the other side of the coin, there were people in all those same countries who agreed that what Hitler and the Nazis were doing was wrong but simply kept their heads down and tried to weather the storm without doing anything to fight it. They sat in their houses and perhaps talked about how they disagreed with what was going on around them but refused to speak out in public or actively participate in any resistance.

Can you imagine living in a time and place where it seems like everyone around you is either participating in evil or closing their eyes to it and refusing to get involved? Perhaps, if you think about it, you don't have to imagine hard at all. Evil may not parade around wearing special armbands. And it's usually not as simple as being able to blame it on one person, one government, or one agenda. But it is there. It is everywhere. It is marching relentlessly forward into homes, families, and lives around the world. It is subtle and sometimes hard to recognize. It can seem desirable and make us feel like we belong. It can make us afraid to resist it.

When I read the stories of courageous resistance fighters, I often ask myself if I would have participated in the resistance if I had lived back then. And, inevitably, I answer, "Well, I like to think that I would have." Of course I think that! Looking back at those horrific events, the right thing to do seems pretty obvious. But then I have to ask myself, "Am I doing my part NOW, to stand against the evil of my time? Am I standing for truth whenever I have the chance—not just in my home where it's safe? Am I helping those around me? Am I tireless in my efforts to spread light and truth? Or, am I sitting safely in my house, talking about what's wrong with the world, instead of actually doing something about it? The truth of the matter is, if we don't stand firm in the small tests of life, we will not stand firm in the large ones.

When you look back on your life, which person do you want to see in yourself? The one who did whatever they could to resist evil, no matter how small, or the one who recognized the evil in the world and felt sad about it but who, ultimately, did nothing to fight it?

We know that God's goodness will ultimately triumph. We know whose side is going to win. The only question we need to ask ourselves is whose side are we going to be on? We are either for the Lord or against Him because, unlike World War II, there is no neutral territory in the war against evil.

Standing for truth isn't always easy, but this training manual will help you overcome your fears, doubts, and any other challenges that stand in your way. As you read and practice the principles taught here, you will grow in faith, and gain the skills you need to become a powerful and effective resistance agent in the Lord's army.

Will you join us?

—Kathryn Moss

A PORTRAIT IN COURAGE: RUDI WOBBE

"I'm kind of glad that in my youth I was shaken hard to come to my senses, to realize what life is all about; that there are more important things in life than just to be entertained and to have a good time. There are responsibilities. There are obligations. Would I do it all the same again? YES. I stand up for whatever is right and just and fair—WHEREVER THERE IS ANYTHING OF DISREPUTE, I STAND MY GROUND."

RUDI WOBBE (1926–1992): *Member of The Hübener Group—three German teenagers who secretly typed up anti-Nazi leaflets and distributed them around Hamburg. For six months Rudi and his friends, Helmuth Hübener and Karl-Heinz Schnibbe, managed to distribute hundreds of leaflets by stuffing them in mailboxes, telephone booths and even pinning them to Nazi party bulletin boards! In February of 1942 they were betrayed by a co-worker. Rudi was arrested just a few days after his sixteenth birthday and was sentenced to ten years in a labor camp.* (Read more about the Hübener Group on pg. 147)

SECTION 1:

RECRUITMENT

"The only difference between ordinary and extraordinary are the actions you decide to take."

—Anonymous

STEP INTO YOUR PLACE

1. THE RESISTANCE NEEDS YOU!

You may be thinking, "Why me? I'm not smart enough, strong enough, or brave enough; I don't have the support others have, or the health, or the money, or the faith to really make a difference. I don't have any special talents. What could I possibly do that others couldn't do better?"

Some of the biggest obstacles we face are the limits we place on ourselves. For some reason we think we have to be someone or something different than we are in order to make a difference or do anything important.

When I was researching which school I wanted to attend for my graduate training, I came across a program at the University of London, in England. It sounded like it was just what I was looking for and I couldn't help thinking how awesome it would be to go to school in a different country. I remember one night talking to my husband and telling him about the program. Laughing, I said, "It sure would be nice to be able to go to school in London." My husband just looked at me and said, "Why not do it?" I sat there for a second and couldn't think of anything to say. I had no good answer to that. Sure, it would take a lot of work and there would many things to arrange and take care of, but as I thought about it, I realized that there was no real reason I couldn't apply and go except that for some reason I had subconsciously ruled it out as something too cool for me. It seemed like the kind of thing that other people do—people who are richer or more world savvy, or more confident than me. I said, "We couldn't seriously move to London for a couple years, could we?" Again, his response was, "Why not?"

> The Lord doesn't use the most talented, gifted, rich or confident people to accomplish His purposes. He uses those who will ask for His help and recognize His hand in the results.

Because of my husband's question, I realized that I had been holding myself back! I didn't really think of it as a possibility for myself. It seemed so far out of my reach that I hadn't even seriously considered it. So, I applied for the graduate program and got accepted, and we moved to London and had one of the most fantastic experiences of our lives. Since that time, I have been much more aware of when I may be holding myself back. I have continued to ask myself "why not?" and it has led to more growth and joy than I could have ever imagined. I will be forever grateful to my husband for asking that one simple question.

It is Satan, the father of all lies, who wants you to feel like you aren't capable of much. He wants you to feel small, hopeless, weak and worthless. But, my friends, it is a LIE! It is perhaps the most devious and powerful and incorrect of all lies! Because YOU are a child of God, and through faith in Jesus Christ, you have power beyond imagining!

When the Lord commanded Moses to lead the Israelites out of Egypt, there were 600,000 men on foot and all the women and children besides that. So we're talking roughly a million people. This was no small task! Was Moses an experienced leader at this point? No. Was he a top-notch wilderness guide, well trained in the art of wilderness survival? Nope. Was he a powerful and charismatic person that everyone naturally listened to? No, again! In fact, he was a terrible speaker. He even told the Lord that he was painfully "slow of speech."

When we think of Moses, we think of all the incredible miracles to come: the plagues of Egypt, parting the Red Sea, the Ten Commandments, and leading the Israelites for forty years! But he had no idea that any of that was coming. When Moses was first called by the Lord he said, "Who am I that I should go unto Pharaoh, and that I should bring forth the children of Israel out of Egypt?" (Exodus 3:11). In other words, "Why me? I'm just a nobody. I'm sure there is someone else who can do this better."

But the Lord doesn't judge us the way we judge ourselves! He tells us that while we may judge ourselves, and others, on outward appearances or worldly achievements, He judges us by our hearts (1 Samuel 16:7). He can see our honest, and sincere desires. And most importantly, He can see what we are capable of becoming if we will trust Him.

My friends, you may say to yourself, "But I can't do that! I can't make a difference or do anything big or important." But I say to you,

WHY NOT?

FROM THE BIBLE: FACING A GIANT

Let no man's heart fail because of him; [I] thy servant will go and fight with this Philistine.

—1 Samuel 17:32

IN THE BOOK OF SAMUEL, WE read about a young shepherd named David. When he was a teenager, there was war between the Israelites and the Philistines, but David wasn't old enough to join the army.

As the two armies faced each other, the Philistines sent their champion forward. Goliath was over nine feet tall and was a strong and seasoned fighter. He stood shouting challenges and insults to the nervous Israelite army. When David, who had come to bring his brothers food, heard Goliath and saw that everyone else was too afraid to face him, David volunteered to fight the giant himself!

Can't you just hear the laughter and see the disbelief on the men's faces when they saw this young, inexperienced kid say he would defeat such a terrifying opponent? Even Goliath, when he saw David, thought this was some kind of a joke. He taunted David, telling him that animals will soon be feeding on his dead body. Unfazed, David stood his ground, and shouted back, "Thou comest to me with a sword, with a spear, and with a shield: but I

Behold also the ships, which though they be so great . . . yet are they turned about with a very small helm.

—James 3:4

come to thee in the name of the Lord of hosts. . . . This day will the Lord deliver thee into mine hand." (1 Samuel 17:45–46)

Furious, Goliath pulled out his sword and started towards David, but David calmly put a stone in his sling, and unleashed it at the angry giant. The stone struck Goliath right in the forehead and killed him. The Israelite army was triumphant, and young David was suddenly a hero!

God does not use the powerful and mighty Goliaths to accomplish His purposes. He uses the humble Davids; those who turn to Him for help, and those who will give the glory to God for all the miracles that will follow. David later became a great leader, but he was a young, inexperienced shepherd when he slew Goliath. Moses was a terrible speaker, and felt insecure about his abilities, and yet he ended up performing incredible miracles and leading the Israelites out of Egypt. Do you see what I mean? They were regular people, just like you—but with God, they did extraordinary things!

My friends, you do not need to be the tallest, the strongest, the smartest, or the most powerful in order to fight for the kingdom of God. In fact, your talents and abilities have little to do with it at all. The only thing required to fight in God's army is a desire to do so. If you have a sincere desire to fight against the evil around you and stand for truth and goodness, God will help you with everything else!

> But God hath chosen the foolish things of the world to confound the wise; and God hath chosen the weak things of the world to confound the things which are mighty.
>
> —1 Corinthians 1:27

TALK ABOUT IT!

1. When David was going to face Goliath, the king offered him armor to wear, but David refused it and took only his sling. Why do you think he was able to do that? Do you have the faith to face the giants in your life with the Lord as your only armor?

2. God could have freed the Israelites himself, but He didn't. Why do you think God uses us to accomplish his purposes, when He could just make the miracles happen without us?

3. What are some ways you hold yourself back from doing things? Why do you think we do that to ourselves? What can you do to overcome that?

HARRIET TUBMAN: FROM SLAVE TO FREEDOM FIGHTER

"'Twant me, 'twas the Lord. I always told him, 'I trust to you. I don't know where to go or what to do, but I expect you to lead me,' and He always did."

—Harriet Tubman

IN 1822, ARAMINTA ROSS, BETTER KNOWN AS HARRIET TUBMAN, was born into slavery on a plantation in Maryland. According to the laws of the time, she had no rights at all. She was considered the property of her owners and they could do with her as they wished. She couldn't own property, be educated, or even conduct business without the agreement of her owners.

When Harriet was a teenager, she was struck in the head with a two-pound weight for refusing to help capture a runaway slave. The injury was severe, and as a result, she suffered from horrible headaches, seizures and narcoleptic episodes for the rest of her life.

In 1849 Harriet made a daring escape from slave life and fled to the North. Trusting in God to guide her, she traveled on foot for ninety miles before she finally arrived in Philadelphia and claimed her freedom. Harriet could have rested, enjoying her freedom, but she chose to return to the South again and again to help rescue other slaves and bring them to freedom. Over the next eleven years, Harriet made around nineteen trips there and back, helping rescue hundreds of slaves, bringing them north through a secret network of safe houses, known as the Underground Railroad. In fact, she brought so many slaves to freedom, the people began to call her Moses! During the American Civil War, Harriet worked as an armed scout and a spy for the Union army. She even led the Combahee River Raid, which freed seven hundred slaves.

After the war ended, Harriet dedicated the rest of her life to helping impoverished former slaves and the elderly. She was never financially secure herself, but she donated what she had whenever she could to help those around her.

Harriet Tubman was not born to privilege. She was a slave. She wasn't educated, and didn't have much money. By the world's standards she did not have much, and yet because of her faith and humility, God was able to use her to do a mighty work!

TRY IT!

- Take time this week to ask Heavenly Father if He knows you.

- Ask Him if He has a special work for you to do!

- And ask Him to help you figure out what that is. I promise He will answer.

- He may not answer right away or in the way you are thinking— but He will answer!

- Write down the thoughts and feelings you have.

2. YOU'RE HERE FOR A REASON

Stars form inside dense concentrations of interstellar gas and dust. In the extreme cold the gases become molecular and the atoms begin to bind together. When the density reaches a certain point, a star forms. The whole process from gas to star is said to take millions of years.

That means that for the star of Bethlehem to appear at the exact right time, announcing the birth of the Savior, it had to begin its journey millions of years beforehand. It had to be placed in its orbit long before Mary was to deliver Jesus; long before she was visited by the angel; long before she was even born, or the Savior's birth was prophesied. It means that the events that created that star had to be set in motion millions of years before it was ever needed.

It's mind-blowing and incredible, isn't it? Don't you think that if God could do that with a star, He could do it with you? Think about that for a minute. Events were set in motion long before you were ever born that will put you right where you need to be at the exact time you are needed.

While I was writing the screenplay for my film, *Resistance Movement*, I began having dreams that something important was missing from it. It had something to do with one of the main characters. I prayed that I would be led to discover what it was. Since it was a true story, I began doing more research about the true-life person I was writing about to see if I could figure out what was missing. As I was researching, I discovered there was an old German play that this particular person loved and often quoted from. I had no idea where to find this obscure play, but I knew I needed to read it.

THINK ABOUT THIS:

You have a purpose in life. If you didn't, you would already be dead!

A few days later, I was at the thrift store and, on a whim, decided to walk through the book section to see if there was anything interesting. As I walked through, I glanced down, and there, in the thrift store, in the middle of Utah, was a copy of that very play! I couldn't believe it! It was an old copy that had been printed in the early 1950's, and it had the name of its first owner written on the inside flap.

I bought it, took it home and read it immediately. As I read, the answer to my dream became clear and I knew what my play had been missing. I was so grateful. As I knelt in prayer to thank Heavenly Father for this great blessing of inspiration and guidance, I was struck with a powerful realization: This book didn't just suddenly appear when I needed it. The events that brought that book to the place I needed it at the precise time I needed it had been set in motion years and years before I ever uttered that prayer. Someone back in the 1950s had to purchase the book. They had to hold onto it until just the right time, decide to donate it to charity, and donate it in the exact right place and at that exact time for me to find it. In other words, the Lord knew what I needed before I even knew it myself, and He set things in motion years before so the answer I sought would be ready for me at the exact time and place I needed it.

As these thoughts flooded my mind, I felt such a strong sense of love and peace. I knew this was not just an isolated incident. This is how the Lord works! He knows what we will need long before we even know we need it. He also knows what we are capable of and who will need our help long before we do. And He places us, and others, exactly where and when we are needed; in the right place at the right time.

There is nothing accidental about your being alive at this time. You are here for a specific purpose and you have been given the exact gifts and experiences needed to make a difference in a way that no one else can. You were born for such a time as this!

How cool is it that the same God who created sunsets and oceans and galaxies, thought the world needed one of you!

FROM THE BIBLE: FOR SUCH A TIME AS THIS

For how can I endure to see the evil that shall come unto my people? Or how can I endure to see the destruction of my kindred?

—Esther 8:6

IN THE PERSIAN EMPIRE, around 485 BC, there was a young Jewish girl named Esther. She had been chosen by King Ahasuerus to be his new queen. When Esther was chosen to go to the palace, her guardian and cousin, Mordecai, told her not to tell anyone that she was Jewish because it could be dangerous. There was a powerful man in the kingdom named Haman who hated the Jewish people. Haman went to the king and convinced him to kill all the Jews in the kingdom because they were a danger to his power. When Mordecai learned of this he went to Esther and begged her to try to change the king's mind.

Esther was terrified. This wasn't a small or easy thing Mordecai was asking her to do. King Ahasuerus was strict with the rules governing his court and harsh in his punishments. She could only go to him when he specifically asked for her. He hadn't asked to see her for over a month and, if she entered his presence without being asked, she could be killed. Seeing Esther's hesitation, Mordecai told her that if she remained silent, God would send the Jews deliverance through someone else, but that she and her family would perish. Finally, he asked, "Who knoweth whether thou art come to the kingdom for such a time as this?" (Esther 4:14)

Esther agreed to try approaching the king if the Jewish people would join her in fasting and prayer for three days first. After the days of fasting ended, Esther made herself ready. She dressed in her finest clothes and made herself as beautiful as she could. Then, with a pounding heart, she entered the king's chamber. She must have stood there for what felt like an eternity, waiting to see if the king would accept her presence or condemn her to death for her intrusion. At last, the king raised his golden scepter and accepted her presence.

Through a series of feasts, Esther told the king that she was a Jew and asked for her people to be protected. King Ahasuerus ordered the extermination order to be revoked. Not only that, but the Jews were also given protection and the freedom to live their religion and fight against anyone who tried to take their rights from them. All because Esther had the faith to recognize that God had placed her in this position at the exact time she was needed.

> Arise; for this matter belongeth unto thee: . . .
> Be of good courage, and do it.
> —Ezra 10:4

TALK ABOUT IT!

1. What are some of the strengths you see in yourself? What makes you unique?

2. Why do you think God wanted you to be born in this particular time and place?

3. Mordecai told Esther that if she kept silent, the Lord would save His people through someone else, but that she and her family would miss out on the blessings and suffer for refusing. How often do we miss out on blessings because we are too afraid to do what the Lord asks of us?

ROSA PARKS: THE WOMAN WHO SPARKED A MOVEMENT

"God has always given me the strength to say what is right."

—Rosa Parks

ROSA LOUISE PARKS LIVED IN AMERICA DURING THE TIME OF RACIAL segregation. There were laws stating that white people and black people could not share the same restrooms or drinking fountains and that on buses the black passengers would have to sit in the back, reserving the front seats for the white passengers.

On December 1, 1955 Rosa boarded the bus home after a long day of work in a Montgomery, Alabama department store. A few stops later, the white section of the bus was full so the bus driver told Rosa and three other African American passengers to stand and give up their seats to the white passengers who had just boarded. The three others reluctantly stood, but Rosa was tired. She was tired from working on her feet all day, but even more than that she was tired of continually giving in. And so Rosa Parks refused to stand and give up her seat. She was consequently arrested, sparking a bus boycott that lasted 382 days and thrusting her in the spotlight as the "Mother of the Freedom Movement."

She said later,

"I did not want to be mistreated; I did not want to be deprived of a seat that I had paid for. It was just time . . . there was an opportunity for me to take a stand to express the way I felt about being treated in that manner. I had not planned to get arrested. I had plenty to do without having to end up in jail. But when I had to face that decision, I didn't hesitate to do so because I felt that we had endured that too long. The more we gave in, the more we complied with that kind of treatment, the more oppressive it became."

Rosa Parks was exactly where she needed to be, at the time when so many needed someone to have the courage to stand against racism. She was placed in that situation at that time, because the Lord knew she would have the courage to do what she felt needed to be done.

YOUR SPARK CAN BECOME A FLAME AND CHANGE EVERYTHING!

TRY IT!

- Think of something wonderful that happened to you, or think of a good friend that you've met.

- Think back on all the events and circumstances that led to that meeting or experience—the things that would have stopped you from meeting if they had been different.

- Make a list and follow the chain of events as far back as you can!

- Note the many ways you can see God's hand in leading you to that experience.

3. THE COURAGE TO BEGIN

When I traveled to Italy, I was part of a large group being shown around by a local guide. After a while, we reached a busy street that we needed to cross. When I approached the curb, the guide, along with half the group, had already crossed to the other side. I stood there, waiting patiently for traffic to stop so I, along with the other half of the group, could cross the street safely. But guess what? Traffic didn't stop. The cars just kept zooming by without even slowing down.

After some time, our guide looked back to see where we were and realized that we were still waiting to cross the road. He turned to us and shouted, "Don't wait for the cars to stop! Step into the street first and then the way will clear!"

WHAT?! He wanted us to step into the busy street, and trust that the cars would stop in time? That sounded crazy–especially because I was the one in front of the group and everyone else was waiting for me to step into the traffic first.

My heart was pounding, as everyone looked at me expectantly. Finally, after a quick prayer, I took a deep breath, and stepped off the curb into the busy street. To my amazement—and great relief—the traffic all around me stopped and we were able to cross the road safely.

The Lord often works in the same way. Sometimes He stops the traffic first and it's immediately clear what He wants us to do and when we should do it. Sometimes we see clearly the talents He has given us and the ways He wants us to use them. However, sometimes God wants us to take the first step by choosing for ourselves and moving forward without clear direction from Him. In other words, He expects us to have faith. Sometimes it is only after we take those first steps that the way is made clear before us. He expects us to use the brains and talents He has given us to decide what to do. And then He expects us to step off the curb and begin.

Don't wait for a major revelation of your life's purpose; the Lord will make the way clear as you move forward.

FROM THE BIBLE: JUMP OFF THE BOAT!

If ye suffer for righteousness' sake, happy are ye. And be not afraid, . . . neither be troubled. . . .

For it is better, if the will of God be so, that ye suffer for well doing, than for evil doing.

—1 Peter 3:14, 17

AFTER THE CRUCIFIXION AND RESurrection of the Savior, Peter, along with John and a few other disciples, were out fishing on the Sea of Galilee. They had been fishing all night and hadn't caught a single fish!

When morning came, a man stood on the shore and asked them if they had caught anything. They said no, and he told them to cast their nets over the other side of the boat.

When they did so, they pulled up nets full to overflowing with fish. Seeing this, John said that the man on the shore was the Lord. When Peter heard this, he immediately wrapped his cloak around himself, jumped into the sea and swam toward the shore and the Savior.

He did not stop to think, "Wait a minute—that water might be cold." He did not talk himself out of it by justifying that he could just wait and arrive at the shore soon enough by staying on the boat. He didn't question the depth of the water or what might be in it. He simply saw the Savior and leaped! (See John 21:1–7.)

You may be thinking, but that sounds hard or scary. Well, it might be. But so what? Can't you do hard things? Aren't you brave enough to do something that makes you feel nervous? Satan tries to use your fears to stop you from reaching your full potential and doing good in the world. Show him that you refuse to give in! The truth is that doing something new might feel a bit uncomfortable for a while. You might want to retreat to the comfort and familiarity of the boat or the sidewalk, but don't do it! Just keep going and it will get easier!

> Be strong and of a good courage, fear not . . . for the Lord thy God, He it is that doth go with thee; he will not fail thee, nor forsake thee.
>
> —Deuteronomy 31:6

The joy and fulfillment you will experience when you join the Lord's army and do your part to stand for truth will far outweigh your momentary fears.

Be brave! Take the leap!

TALK ABOUT IT!

1. What can these two examples teach us about facing our fears?

2. What are some things you've done in the past that you were nervous or scared to do?

3. How did you feel after facing your fears and doing them anyway?

SOPHIE SCHOLL: TRUE COURAGE

"The real damage is done by those millions who want to 'survive.' Those who don't like to make waves—or enemies. It's the reductionist approach to life: if you keep it small, you'll keep it under control. But it's all an illusion, because they die too, those people who roll up their spirits into tiny little balls so as to be safe. Life is always on the edge of death; narrow streets lead to the same place as wide avenues, and a little candle burns itself out just like a flaming torch does. I choose my own way to burn."

—Sophie Scholl

SOPHIA MAGDALENA SCHOLL WAS A STUDENT AT THE UNIVERSITY OF Munich and was active within the White Rose non-violent resistance group in Nazi Germany. The White Rose was made up of her brother, Hans, and several of their university friends, including Willi Graf, Alexander Schmorell, Christoph Probst, and Kurt Huber, who was one of their professors. The group secretly typed up leaflets to inspire the German people to stand against Hitler. They made hundreds of copies on a small mimeograph machine and then mailed them all over Germany.

On February 18, 1943, Sophie and Hans were caught spreading copies of one of their leaflets on the University campus and were handed over to the Gestapo. Four days later, after enduring multiple interrogations they were on trial before the infamous Nazi court known as the "Blood Tribunal."

Reports of the interrogations and trial reveal the courage of this small girl standing before the power of the Nazi regime. They were determined to crush her, but she never flinched, never cried, and never wavered. Sophie boldly declared her beliefs to the end saying, "Somebody, after all, had to make a start. What we wrote and said is also believed by many others. They just don't dare express themselves as we did."

At the end of the trial, Sophie and Hans, along with Christoph Probst, who had also been arrested, were convicted of high treason and sentenced to death. They were beheaded by guillotine that same day.

> Courage doesn't mean you don't feel afraid. True courage is deciding that something else is more important than your fear.

It wasn't that Sophie wasn't afraid. Several of her personal letters and diary entries from this time talked about how she was filled with fear and uncertainty. She wanted to live. She wanted to be carefree and not have to worry about everything that was going on. But there was something she wanted more. She was willing to face her fears because more than any of those other things, Sophie wanted to be free.

We will not be silent!

—The White Rose

TRY IT!

- What is one small thing you can do to start making the world a better place?

- How can you take the first step TODAY?

- Say a prayer for help and courage and then step off the curb!

- Jump off the boat and DO IT!

4. COMMITTING TO THE CAUSE

A number of years ago, I became involved in martial arts. I had never tried it before, but I absolutely loved it! I wanted to practice all the time and couldn't wait for each class! And when the time came to sign the pledge stating that I would commit to earn my black belt, I eagerly signed my name.

For several months after that, things went really well. I felt good about what I was accomplishing and how I was improving. Then one day, I suddenly injured my right shoulder. I rested it for a time, but it wouldn't heal. I continued going to my classes, but I had to just sit and watch because of my injured shoulder. I hated it.

> Commitment means staying loyal to what you said you were going to do long after the mood you said it in has left you.

One day, I was so discouraged and frustrated I didn't even want to go to class. I thought I would rather sit out at home than have to sit out at class and watch everyone moving on without me. But, as I was thinking about it, a distinct thought came to my mind; "If you do not go to class tonight, somewhere along the way, you will end up quitting." It struck me powerfully, and I did go to class that night even though I didn't feel like it. After all, I had committed to see this through, and I meant it.

So, time passed and my shoulder stubbornly refused to heal. I ended up needing surgery, which forced me to take even more time off. However, I was hopeful that, after the surgery healed, my shoulder problems would finally be over, and I could continue with my training in the way I wanted to.

The surgery did heal, but just a couple months after I was able to fully participate again, my other shoulder began to hurt. Again, I had to rest, hold back and sit out. I was frustrated, but eventually, with time and therapy, it got better, and I was able to get on with my training.

But then I injured my knee. And after that healed, I broke my big toe. After that healed, I hurt my hip; then, my other hip. Then I had four discs slip in my neck. And then it was my knee—again. This went on constantly for four years. I watched the other people in my group move ahead and test for their black belts without me. I was so tired of sitting out, so tired of constantly hurting, so tired of having to hold back.

> I have fought a good fight, I have finished the race, I have kept the faith.
>
> —2 Timothy 4:7 (NKJV)

At this point my discouragement was at an all-time high. In spite of all the effort I had put into it, I was ready to quit. Yes, I had committed to get my black belt, but clearly my body had other plans for me. I had done everything I could, and it wasn't my fault that I wouldn't be able to finish my training. However, as I prayed and thought about what I should do, the pledge that I had signed all those years before came to my mind. I pulled out the paper and read it. It said that I would do whatever it took to get my black belt. Whatever it took. Did I really mean that?

I had to ask myself some difficult questions: Did I really mean I would still get my black belt—even if I had to take twice as long as everyone else? Did I really mean I would stick with it, no matter how many times I was injured and no matter how many times I had to sit out? In other words, did I really mean I would do it—NO MATTER WHAT?

I recommitted once again and resumed my training with renewed determination. Then, a week before my big black belt test, the pain in my knee suddenly returned. I went to the doctor, who did everything he could, I bought a brace, and I prayed and prayed for the strength to complete my test. I felt peaceful and calm and knew that everything was going to be all right. Over the three-day black belt test, my knee did not hurt once, and I was able to do everything I needed to pass my test! It truly was a miracle!

My friends, often we think we have committed to something but have left ourselves a little bit of an "out" just in case. We usually don't even recognize that we're doing it. When I first signed my black belt pledge, I believed I was really committed. It wasn't until things came along to test that commitment, that I realized I wasn't as committed as I thought.

Commitment does not mean, "I commit to loving everyone . . . unless they are hateful, and mean." It doesn't mean, "I commit to praying daily . . . unless I am too tired or busy." It doesn't mean, "I commit to make a difference . . . unless it becomes too hard." And it doesn't mean, "I commit to follow Jesus Christ . . . unless I find something better."

When I finally earned my black belt, after all the struggles, the continuous pain, and countless setbacks, words cannot describe how empowered, grateful, and proud I felt! The lesson I learned during that time was more than just the principles of martial arts. I learned that when we truly commit, we open ourselves up to a real power! That power is faith—faith that God will help us do what He wants us to do. And where there is faith, there are miracles.

ARE YOU TRULY COMMITTED TO
THE GOSPEL OF JESUS CHRIST?

FROM THE BIBLE: WHEREVER YOU GO, I WILL GO

For whither thou goest,
I will go;
and where thou lodgest,
I will lodge;
Thy people shall be my people,
and thy God, my God.

—Ruth 1:16

IN THE OLD TESTAMENT, WE learn the story of Ruth, Naomi, and Orpah. Naomi was an Israelite widow who was living in Moab with her two sons. Each of the sons had married a Moabite woman. One was named Ruth and one was Orpah.

After ten years of marriage, both of Naomi's sons died as well, leaving the three women alone. Naomi decided to head back to her homeland, and both Ruth and Orpah wanted to come with her. However, on the road, Naomi told them that they should go back to Moab and their families. If they came with her they would be alone, living a life of poverty. Both Ruth and Orpah cried and declared that they would rather stay with Naomi. Naomi again told them that they should return to their families because she had nothing to offer them. After thinking about this, Orpah decided to return to Moab, but Ruth refused to leave Naomi.

It's interesting that the scriptures say that Orpah went "back to her people and to her gods." She returned to Moab and to her previous way of life and religion. Ruth, however, told Naomi that she would stay with her no matter where she went; that Naomi's people would become her people and Naomi's God would become her God.

So, what was it that made Ruth to stay with Naomi? At first both women begged to stay with her. Orpah loved Naomi just like Ruth did, so what was the difference? Both Ruth and Orpah were committed to Naomi, but Ruth was also committed to God. We can be committed to many different things and many different people, but it is only commitment to the Lord that will give us the strength to resist every temptation to give up.

When Ruth chose to honor her commitment to Naomi and God, she chose a life of hardship. But God led her and made it possible for her to earn a living, to take care of herself and Naomi, and eventually to remarry.

> If you truly commit to God, He will make it possible for you to accomplish your goals—even if it takes a long time, and many sacrifices to get there.

There have been times throughout history when being a Christian was the easy or popular choice to make. But this is not one of those times. In fact, it's becoming increasingly difficult to be a Christian as the years go by. It's no longer popular or even accepted to believe in Jesus Christ and live His gospel. As this persecution increases, will you find yourself turning back to the safety and comfort of your old ways? Or will you have the commitment, like Ruth, to give up whatever you need to in order to stay true to the Lord?

> Commit thy way unto the Lord; trust also in him; and he shall bring it to pass. And he shall bring forth thy righteousness as the light, and thy judgment as the noonday.
>
> —Psalms 37:5–6

TALK ABOUT IT

1. When we come up against obstacles in our path we can let them stop us, or we can work to overcome them. How does choosing to overcome the obstacles make us stronger?

2. Why do you think God allows us to struggle so much to reach our goals? Would reaching your goals be as special to you, if they came easily?

3. What is it you are truly committed to? Do your actions reflect that?

WILLIAM WILBERFORCE: RELENTLESS COMMITMENT

"Our motto must continue to be perseverance. And ultimately I trust the Almighty will crown our efforts with success."

—William Wilberforce

WILLIAM WILBERFORCE WAS BORN IN HULL, YORKSHIRE, ENGLAND. He was a member of the British Parliament and was known for being charming and also eloquent and witty as a speaker.

In 1784, Wilberforce became an evangelical Christian. His conversion changed the direction of his life. He stopped gambling and drinking, and even for a time considered leaving politics for the church. However, he came to feel that God had called him to accomplish two main tasks: the reformation of society and the abolition of the slave trade. He vowed to do just that.

In 1789 Wilberforce introduced a stunning twelve resolutions to abolish the slave trade. They were all defeated. For over a decade, Wilberforce continued introducing an abolition bill every year. And every year, it continued to be defeated. Each time William Wilberforce introduced his bill, the mocking and complaints grew louder. And yet he continued to try—over and over again. People became angry and annoyed with him. They told him to stop and some even threatened his life. On top of it all, Wilberforce was also battling a health condition we now know as ulcerative colitis. He was sick, tired and discouraged, but he had committed to abolish the slave trade and nothing was going to stand in his way. Wilberforce continued to fight relentlessly for what he believed in. At long last, the bill was finally passed in 1807, twenty years after he first introduced it.

Twenty years! If anyone had just cause to say to themselves, "Well, I tried. I did all I could. It's not my fault the bill won't pass," it was William Wilberforce. And yet, he refused to give up. He kept fighting on and on, no matter what. No matter who opposed him, no matter how others reacted, no matter how long it took.

He worked throughout his life to make the world around him a better place. In spite of all who opposed him and his own physical illness, William Wilberforce relentlessly fought against sin and cruelty wherever he found it.

DECIDE TODAY TO BE RELENTLESS
IN YOUR COMMITMENTS.

TRY IT!

- Take some time today to make a personal commitment to yourself and to God.

- Don't just think it; write it down and sign it! Keep it somewhere safe as a reminder of your commitment.

- Pray to God. Tell Him your desires, and commit to standing for truth and righteousness—no matter what!

A PORTRAIT IN COURAGE: ANDRE & MAGDA TROCMÉ

"Look hard for ways to make little moves against destructiveness . . . These people came here for help and for shelter. I am their shepherd. A shepherd does not forsake his flock."

—Andre Trocmé

ANDRE (1901–1971) & MAGDA TROCMÉ (1901–1996) *Andre served as Pastor in the town of Le Chambon-sur-Lignon. When France fell to the Nazis, Andre and his wife determined to help the Jews in any way they could. Knowing they risked their lives, they opened their home to anyone in need and began hiding Jewish refugees who where fleeing from the Nazis. They encouraged the people of their town to join them and set up a large network of people to help. Together Andre, Magda, and the town they inspired were able to save around 3,500 people from the Gestapo.*

SECTION 2:

BASIC TRAINING

"There are no shortcuts to any place worth going."

—Helen Keller

5. DISCOVERING & DEVELOPING TALENTS

When I was growing up and would compare myself to my older sister, this is what I saw: In her, I saw someone who was confident and patient. I saw someone who loved kids and who was great working with them. I also saw someone who was spiritual and not afraid to try new things. It was not uncommon for women to tell her that they hoped their sons would marry her—or someone just like her. She got accepted into the Gifted and Talented program in elementary school, and in high school she took several advanced placement classes. She was petite and pretty, and friends would fight over who got to walk next to her! In my eyes she was the ideal of what a person should be.

When I looked at myself, I saw none of those things. In myself, I saw someone who hated babysitting and wasn't particularly enthusiastic about having kids in

> Everyone is a genius. But if you judge a fish by its ability to climb a tree, it will live its whole life believing it is stupid.

the future. I saw someone who was impatient, who lacked confidence and was extremely shy. I was very tall and felt awkward. I tested for the Gifted program and didn't get in. No one ever fought over me, and no one told me they wanted their sons to marry me. I discovered I had a talent for theatre and participated in it through out high school, but I felt like my sister had the talents that really mattered.

Then one day, after we were grown, my sister and I were talking, and I shared a bit of what I had felt. And do you know what? She was absolutely stunned because she said that she had always seen my talents for theater and other creative things and felt that I was the one with the "real" talents! I couldn't believe it! We sat there laughing and crying together, surprised and humbled to learn that we each had been comapring ourselves to the other and feeling like the inferior one.

> You're at the start of something great. Don't let another person's progress discourage you.

There is no end to the many different talents and gifts available to us and the ways they can be used to help make the world a better, brighter, more beautiful and wonderful place. In the search for your specific talents, do not compare your gifts to the gifts of others. Do not make the mistake of thinking that you are the one person on this earth who doesn't have any. Some talents may be more obvious than others, but they are all talents, and they are all needed. Remember, if God's plan was for all of us to be exactly the same, He would have made us that way.

FROM THE BIBLE: BURYING YOUR TALENTS

Well done, thou good and faithful servant; thou hast been faithful over a few things, I will make thee ruler over many things.

—Matthew 25:21

IN THE NEW TESTAMENT, JESUS tells of a man who was about to undertake a long journey. Before he left, he divided his money between his servants so they could take care of it while he was gone. He gave five talents to servant #1, two talents to servant #2, and one talent to servant #3.

After the man was gone, the first servant took the five talents he had been given and used them to earn an additional five talents, for a total of ten talents. The second servant took his two talents, engaged in trade, and was also able to double his talents. The third servant was afraid to use the money he had been entrusted with, so he buried it in the ground to keep it safe.

Sometime later, when the man returned from his journey, he asked the three servants what they had done with his money. The first servant showed the man how he had turned the original five talents into ten. The man was very pleased. Then, the second servant showed the man how he too, had doubled the talents he had been given. Again, the man was very pleased. Finally, the man asked the third servant to show what he had done with his money. The third

> It is estimated that one talent was equal to a laborer's pay for around twenty years worth of work! So even the man who was given only one talent, was given a huge gift!

servant was embarrassed that he hadn't made any additional money, but excused himself by saying that he hadn't wanted to take any risks with the money he was given because he didn't want to lose it. The man was angry with the servant for hiding the talent instead of using it to make more money like the others had done. So he took the one talent from him and gave it to the ones who had multiplied their talents.

God has given you talents, and He has not given them to you so you can keep them hidden and safe. He wants you to use your talents; working hard to turn them into even greater abilities and opportunities! Heavenly Father has given you talents so you can bring joy, beauty, love, order, strength and knowledge of all kinds to His children. He wants you to use them to make His army stronger, to bring people to Him and to make the world a better place.

> **Neither do men light a candle, and put it under a bushel, but on a candlestick; and it giveth light unto all that are in the house.**
>
> **—Matthew 5:15**

Rose seeds contain within them all of the DNA they need to become a full-grown flower, but it takes time, care, sunshine, and water for it to develop into a fully grown flower. Just like the rose, you already have within you the seeds of many gifts and talents. Some you are aware of and are developing already, some are still in seed form. Take the time to grow and nurture them, whatever they may be, and be patient with the process.

Does putting yourself out there to use and develop your talents take some risk? Sure! It's hard work developing talents. It can be discouraging and humbling, but I promise you that whatever it takes, it will be worth it. When the Savior returns, looks you in the eye and asks you what you did with the talents He gave you, how glorious it will be to be able to show Him the difference you have made with your gifts. What could be better than to have the Lord smile at you and say, "Well done, good and faithful servant. Thou hast been faithful over a few things. I will make thee ruler over many things. Enter thou into the joy of thy Lord" (Matthew 25:21).

SECTION 2: BASIC TRAINING

That which we persist in doing becomes easier to do, not that the nature of the thing has changed but that our power to do it has increased.

—Ralph Waldo Emerson

TALK ABOUT IT!

1. Why do you think Satan wants you to compare yourself to others?

2. Is there a proper way to look at the gifts and talents of others that doesn't make you feel badly about yourself?

3. Why do you think God makes us work to develop our gifts instead of just giving us natural ability all the time?

GUNDER HÄGG: HARD-WORKING TALENT

"Only hard, intensive, and purposeful training will give good results."

—Gunder Hägg

GUNDER HÄGG LOVED TO RUN AS A TEENAGER IN A REMOTE AREA OF northern Sweden. His father was a woodcutter and Gunder began running or skiing through the woods each day as he helped his father.

One day, his dad wanted to time Gunder to see how fast he was. They set up a course and measured the distance and then Gunder's dad timed his run. His running time was impressive, and Gunder was so inspired by his fast time that he began to train as a runner. He ran through the woods, on the road and anywhere else he could. He ran every day in heat, in rain and in deep snow. He even ran while pulling a sleigh!

Gunder worked hard and by the time he was in his mid twenties, he was winning races and setting world records. Between 1941 and 1945 Gunder set an amazing 15 world records, becoming one of the top runners in the world, and it had all started from that one race in the woods as a teenager. He says that he was inspired by his running time to believe that he had a great talent for running and that belief pushed him to train hard.

It was only years later that Gunder's dad told him he had lied about the run time on that fateful day. He had wanted Gunder to feel like he was doing well and to find a love of running, so he told Gunder his time was much faster than it actually was! It wasn't a natural ability that made Gunder one of the greatest runners in the world—it was his belief in himself, his determination, and his hard work.

> I'm a great believer in luck, and I find the harder I work, the more I have of it.
>
> —Thomas Jefferson

TRY IT!

- Make a list of your strengths and talents. List the ones you feel you currently have and make a list of the ones you want to develop.

- How can you use one of those talents to make the world a better place? What can you do TODAY to get started?

- Choose one talent you would like to develop. Make a plan that will help you achieve your goal.

6. BEING IN TUNE

When I wanted to learn to play the cello, one of the first things I learned was how to tune it. This was important because if it wasn't in tune, it wouldn't matter how correctly I played the notes or how good my technique was, it would still sound terrible.

I remember the first time I got it tuned correctly. It took me a long time and a lot of effort. When I finally got it right, I felt so good and quickly did my best rendition of "Twinkle, Twinkle, Little Star." Then, tired by my efforts, I put the cello away for another day. Life was busy and it was a few days before I got to practice again. I eagerly pulled out the cello, ready to make some music. But guess what? When I began to play Twinkle, Twinkle, Little Star, it sounded wrong. I checked my fingering, I checked the notes, I checked my bow. Everything was correct. I tried it again with no success. It was then that I realized the cello had gone out of tune again!

There is no doubt that a musical instrument needs to be in tune in order to play music that is beautiful and effective. If you tune an instrument just once like I did, it will stay in tune as you play, but if you put it away, it will quickly go out of tune again. I learned that the best way to help your instrument stay in tune is to tune it and play it everyday. As time goes on and your strings settle, and you continue to play it daily, it will only need tiny adjustments to keep it in tune.

So what does this have to do with us? Another definition of the word *instrument* is a tool or object that is used for a particular purpose. We want God to use us to spread the gospel and bless the lives of others, so that makes us the instrument. If we are instruments in the Lord's hands, then what do we need to do to be effective? We need to be in tune!

IN TUNE: In a state in which one thing agrees with, understands or matches another.

Just like musical instruments, we need to have regular tune-ups! We can't have a spiritual feast one day and expect it to last for the rest of our lives. You don't eat one good meal and say, "Okay, now I don't ever have to eat again," so why do we think we can pray and study our scriptures one day and then think it will last us the whole week?

To be in tune with God, we need to agree with and understand Him, His will, and Spirit. Just like the musical instruments, we can be playing the correct notes by trying to do good, but if we are not in tune and following the guidance of the Holy Spirit, our efforts will not be effective. We need to regularly take the time to be still, to ponder, to ask ourselves the difficult questions and have the courage to answer truthfully. And we need to frequently check in and make sure we are continuing to seek and follow His will for us. We need to stay close to the Spirit so that God can more easily speak to and guide us.

FROM THE BIBLE: A JEALOUS KING

Now Saul was afraid of David, because the Lord was with him, and was departed from Saul. . . . And David behaved himself wisely in all his ways; and the Lord was with him.

—1 Samuel 18:12, 14

REMEMBER YOUNG DAVID WHO fought the giant? After he killed Goliath, King Saul was pleased with him and offered David even more responsibility within his army. He went wherever Saul sent him and the Bible tells us he "behaved wisely." David was not only accepted by the people but began to be honored by them as well. One day as David, King Saul, and the Israelite army were returning from battle, the women of the city ran out to meet them. As they ran and danced, they sang, "Saul has slain his thousands and David his ten thousands" (1 Samuel 18:7).

When Saul heard this, he was angry. His pride was hurt and he was jealous of David because the people seemed to like and respect him more than their king. From that day on, King Saul was suspicious of and angry towards David. The scriptures tell us that the Lord "departed from Saul" because of his anger and pride. In other words, he was no longer in tune with the Holy Spirit.

One night, while David was playing music for the king, Saul took the spear in his hand and threw it at David to try and kill him. He wanted to pin him to the wall with it! David escaped, and King Saul continued to try to have him killed in a variety of ways, but the Lord was with David and helped protect him. Unlike Saul, David "acted wisely." In other words, he was obedient and did the things necessary to stay in tune, so the Spirit could help protect him.

A large part of being in tune is keeping ourselves clean and worthy to hear the Spirit of the Lord. God is the light and, if we want to reflect that light and help shine it into the world, we need to keep ourselves clean. Just like a dirty mirror cannot reflect light, the light and truth of God shine through us best when we are spiritually clean and in tune with the Lord.

> Do not have your concert first, and then tune your instrument afterwards. Begin the day with the Word of God and prayer, and get first of all into harmony with Him.
>
> —James Hudson Taylor

TALK ABOUT IT!

1. Is there something in my life that is holding me back from hearing His spirit?

2. Why do you think we can't feel the Spirit when we're angry?

3. What can I do daily to be more in tune with the spirit of God?

4. An instrument goes out of tune because of changes in the environment around it, like temperature and humidity. How does our environment help or hinder us from being in tune with God?

JACQUES LUSSEYRAN: BLIND RESISTANCE FIGHTER

"Light does not come to us from without. Light is in us, even if we have no eyes."

—Jacques Lusseyran

JACQUES LUSSEYRAN WAS BORN SEPTEMBER 19, 1924, IN PARIS, France. One day when Jacques was seven years old, as he was rushing for the door at the end of the school day, someone accidentally shoved him. He fell and hit his head on the sharp corner of the teacher's desk. Pieces of the glasses he was wearing were pushed into his eyes. He lost consciousness and, when he came to, he found he was completely blind in both eyes.

Only a short time later, Jacques realized that even though he could no longer see by looking outward with his eyes, he could "see" if he looked inward. He said there was a light coming from within him and if he paid attention to that light it would show him what was around him. Because he could not see, his other senses became more highly developed, and by being fully present and paying close attention, he learned to sense things around him.

He quickly learned something important about his ability. He came to realize that he could use this gift of inner sight only if he was feeling peace and love. If he was overcome with sadness or fear, he was unable to tap into his inner light and see.

Just after Jacques finished high school, France was invaded by Germany. Within only five weeks, Paris had fallen and was officially occupied by the Nazis. Soon after, Jacques decided he had to do something to help fight for the freedom of his country. He started a resistance group with some friends and they called themselves the Volunteers of Liberty. Their mission was to publish an underground newspaper to help spread the truth. Because of Jacques's incredible ability to see what sighted people could not, he was put in charge of recruitment. It was a vital job because he had to decide which volunteers they could trust and which ones they couldn't. You never knew if the person was sincerely interested in joining the resistance or if they were a spy trying to expose everyone to the Gestapo.

In July 1943, Jacques was betrayed by a fellow resistance worker. He was sent to Buchenwald concentration camp, where he fought to hold onto that inner light and share it with his fellow prisoners. He spent the remainder of the war uplifting and encouraging all those around him in the camp.

In April 1945, Buchenwald was liberated by the Allies, and Jacques was freed. He continued to honor that inner light and went on to become an influential author and professor of French literature.

> But the Comforter, which is the Holy Ghost, whom the Father will send in my name, he shall teach you all things, and bring all thing to your remembrance, whatsoever I have said unto you.
>
> —John 14:26

TRY IT!

- Find a quiet place where you can be alone. Sit or lie down. Close your eyes and be still. Pay attention to the thoughts and feelings that come to you and write down any impressions or thoughts you have.

- Sometimes we have to turn off distractions around us to better hear the Spirit speaking to us. Make a list of some distractions you can clear from your life.

7. DARE TO STAND ALONE

My great-grandpa Arthur was born in 1892. He was pretty wild when he was young, drinking and swearing and causing trouble. Then one day he met a beautiful young lady named Amy. He soon fell completely in love and asked her to be his wife. Amy loved him in return but was adamant that she would only marry him if he gave up his drinking and other wild ways. Arthur solemnly promised her that he would.

Not long after their marriage, Arthur went on a hunting trip with some of his buddies. This had been a tradition for years and he always looked forward to it. After setting up camp his buddies began to drink, which was also a tradition.

It's better to walk alone than to walk with a crowd headed in the wrong direction.

Soon his friends began to notice that Arthur wasn't drinking and urged him to join them. He refused, telling them of his promise to his wife. They left him alone for a while, but as his friends became more drunk, they became more insistent that he drink with them. Finally, they became angry and offended that he wasn't drinking.

They decided that they were going to force him to drink with them. Three or four of them grabbed Arthur and wrestled him to the ground. They tried to force his mouth open so they could pour the liquor down his throat. Arthur refused to open his mouth, clenching his teeth tightly.

Finally, one of his buddies became so angry that he went over to their truck and retrieved a tire iron with a sharp pointed end. He brought it over and was determined to force it through Arthur's clenched teeth and pry his mouth open. At this critical point, Arthur suddenly blurted out: "Boys, boys! If I take one good drink will you let me alone and never bother me about it again?"

His friends agreed and let him go. Arthur dusted himself off, picked up his tin cup, went over to their supply of water, dipped the cup in, lifted it to his mouth and took a long drink.

"Boys," he said. "That is what I call one good drink."

My great-grandpa said that his friends were stunned when they realized how they had been outwitted, but they held to their promise and didn't pressure him to drink anymore. "Neither," said Arthur relating the story, "did I ever go hunting with them again."

Next time you are tempted to go along with the crowd, ask yourself this question:

"Am I doing this to make God happy, or to make others happy?"

FROM THE BIBLE: ALONE AGAINST THE CROWD

In God I have put my trust; I will not be afraid. What can man do to me?

—Psalms 56:11
(NKJV)

NOAH LIVED DURING A TIME when the earth was filled with wickedness. The Lord told him that He would flood the earth and that if Noah and his family wanted to be saved they must build an ark to keep them afloat in the flood that would come.

Noah tried to tell the others in the land. He tried to convince them that they too could be saved if they would repent. But the people didn't listen. In fact, they made fun of him and told him he was a fool. Every single person refused to believe him and treated him like an idiot for building the ark and believing that the earth would be flooded.

I often wonder if Noah had moments of doubt. After all, there was no rain the entire time he was planning and building the ark. He began to gather the animals and still there was no rain. There had certainly never been a world-wide flood or anything even close to suggest that it was possible. He and his family were the only ones who believed it, while the edu-cated, wealthy, influential people all around him did not. Who was

Wrong is wrong, even if everyone else is doing it. Right is right, even if no one else is doing it.

Noah to think that he knew better than everyone else? And yet, he stood firm. He was able to do so because he had the promise of the Lord that the flood would come and the only people who would be saved would be those on the ark. The odds of thousands of people to one don't seem promising, and yet we know that Noah was right, and everybody else was wrong.

We talk about safety in numbers, and there can be. We can find great strength in supporting and protecting one another. But we must be careful not to assume that means that whatever the majority of people are doing must be right. If Noah had thought that, he never would have had the determination to build the ark. We must strengthen our testimonies to the point that even if the whole rest of the world told us we were wrong, we could still believe.

It doesn't matter if a lot of people join you in your quest to live the gospel and make a positive difference in the world, or if every other person on the planet laughs at you and calls you a fool for trying. God has promised you that if you follow him, you will be protected—just like Noah on the ark and Arthur with his buddies.

> Fear thou not; for I am with thee: be not dismayed; for I am thy God: I will strengthen thee; yea, I will help thee; yea, I will uphold thee with the right hand of my righteousness.
>
> —Isaiah 41:10

TALK ABOUT IT!

1. Why do you think we worry about what others think of us more than we worry about what God thinks of us?

2. Why is it important that Arthur never hung out with those particular friends again?

3. How would the story have ended differently if Arthur gave in to his friends?

ERIC LIDDELL: RUNNING FOR GOD

"We are all missionaries. Wherever we go we either bring people nearer to Christ or we repel them from Christ."

—Eric Liddell

ERIC LIDELL, ALSO KNOWN AS THE "FLYING SCOTSMAN," WAS A runner and a Christian missionary. He was a member of the 1924 British Olympic team and was highly favored to win the hundred-meter race in the Paris Olympics. He was Scotland's fastest sprinter and a national hero. He seemed poised for success. However, just a short time before the Olympics, Eric was told that the hundred-meter race would be run on Sunday.

Eric had always believed that Sunday was a day to worship and honor God and he did not participate in work or sports on that day. Eric told the Olympic committee that he would not be participating in the hundred-meter race.

The backlash and the pressure to change his mind were intense. The newspapers and the British people were furious, and some even called him a traitor. However, Eric stood firm and refused to run on Sunday—not even for an Olympic gold medal. He decided to run in the four-hundred-meter race instead, even though his best time in that race was not great, and no one expected him to win.

The four-hundred-meter race was held on the morning of July 11, 1924, and Eric, to the surprise of everyone, ended up winning the gold medal. Not only that, but his time was so good he broke both the Olympic and World records!

Eric returned to Great Britain a hero, and the newspapers and people who were so unkind to him just a short time ago were now scrambling to outdo each other in their praise of him. However, Eric, only concerned with living his life in a way that would honor the principles he believed in, gave up running and dedicated the rest of his life to missionary work in China.

> Never give in, never give in, never, never, never, never—
> in nothing, great or small, large or petty—never give in
> except to convictions of honor and good sense.
>
> —Winston Churchill

TRY IT!

- The friends we choose to hang out with have a huge impact on our choices. Make a list of your friends. Ask yourself: Do my friends help me make good choices? Do they support me in my standards and faith?

- Make a list of the ways you can be a more uplifting influence on the people around you.

8. PRINCIPLES OF SACRIFICE

When I was in high school, my dream was to be a professional actor. I checked out all the acting books I could find in the library and did my best to teach myself everything in them. I tried out for every play I could, and when I got cast I did everything in my power to be the best I could be.

When I was a Junior in High School, the school was putting on a really fun play. There was only a small cast and one of the parts in it was perfect for me. My theatre teacher had already talked with me about it, and I knew that if I auditioned the part would be mine.

There was just one problem. The part I wanted had one line at the end of the play that had some language in it that I did not want to say because of my religious commitments. I decided to talk to my teacher about it and see if we could change the words to something else. I believed in miracles and I knew I was trying to do what was right. I prayed so hard that she would be understanding and let me change the words, but she didn't. The line was a comedic line and if we changed the words she said it wouldn't be as funny. That part was the only one available to me, and my options were to take the role and say the words, or not be in the play at all. I told her I would not be auditioning. Then I went home and cried.

A short time later, there was the chance to audition for a community play with a great part for me, but some of the performances would be on Sundays, and I had promised Heavenly Father I would not work on Sundays. Again, I prayed for a miracle and then went to the director and asked if any exceptions could be made. Again, the answer was no. Again, I watched my friends participate without me.

> What appears today to be a sacrifice will prove instead to be the greatest investment you will ever make.
>
> —Gordon B. Hinckley

I was frustrated. I knew that God could provide a way for me to participate in the plays and still keep my standards, so why was he asking this sacrifice of me? Why would He give me these talents and a strong love for acting, only to take away all my chances to participate?

It was years later that I realized it was because He loves me! He loves me more than I love theatre, more than my desire to participate in those plays, even more than I love Him. Sacrifice means to give up something you want or value for something even more important. Like in chess when you allow your opponent to take your pawn or other less valuable piece in order to protect your king. Or in baseball when the batter bunts the ball and gets out on purpose in order to let other runners advance to the next base.

I wanted to participate in those plays so, so badly. At the time, I was pretty sure that participating in those plays would make me happy. And I've no doubt I would have had a fun time. But thankfully, God knew that learning to trust Him would bring me even greater joy, a joy that would last so much longer than the applause I craved.

When the sacrifices God asks of you seem too hard to bear, remember that Jesus Christ, who is the ultimate example of sacrifice, suffered and died for us, not because he wanted to suffer so much pain, not because it was easy, but because his love for us was greater than his desire for comfort and safety for himself. Sacrifice is hard. It is meant to be hard; that is the whole point. If it's too easy then it isn't a sacrifice. Sacrifice helps us learn to let go of our immediate desires and trust God's vision for us. Without it, we cannot become the person God knows we can become.

ARE YOU WILLING TO SACRIFICE WHO YOU ARE FOR WHO THE LORD CAN HELP YOU BECOME?

FROM THE BIBLE: THE GREATEST TEST

Because thou hast done this thing, and hast not withheld thy son, thine only son . . . In thy seed shall all the nations of the earth be blessed; because thou hast obeyed my voice.

—Genesis 22:16–18

ABRAHAM AND HIS WIFE HAD wanted a child for years. Finally, they were miraculously blessed with a son whom they named him Isaac. They loved Isaac and were so grateful for the blessing of being his parents. He was the joy of their lives. When Isaac was a young man, the Lord told Abraham to go up into the mountain and offer a sacrifice. Abraham was happy to do this. He had done it many times before, offering up an unblemished lamb or other animal as a symbol of how Jesus Christ would make the ultimate sacrifice for us. However, this time things were different. The Lord told Abraham that instead of a lamb, the sacrifice would be the thing he loved most in this world—his precious son, Isaac.

Can you imagine how Abraham must have felt? He had prayed and waited, and waited and prayed for years, asking God for a child. He was finally blessed with the desire of his heart, and now the Lord was asking him to give that up!

Be willing to give up what you want now, for what you want most!

With a heavy heart, Abraham made the preparations and went up into the mountain with Isaac. He bound his son and put him on the altar. I am sure that as he raised the knife over Isaac his hand was shaking and tears were falling. Then, in one of the greatest last-minute saves in the scriptures, just as Abraham was about to slay Isaac, an angel appeared and commanded him to stop. The angel told Abraham that this was a test and that the Lord did not actually want him to kill his son. He then told Abraham that because of his willingness to sacrifice what he loved most, even though he didn't understand why it was necessary, the Lord would bless him and his posterity forever.

The Lord will often ask sacrifices of us. Thankfully, the sacrifices we are asked to make do not require us to sacrifice our family members on an altar. He wants us to sacrifice our will to His. He wants us to sacrifice our time to serve others, our money to help others, our pride to be more humble, our stubbornness to be more faithful. In short, he asks us to sacrifice because that is the only way we can become more like Him. It is the way that His church and kingdom have always been built. Remember, nothing great was ever accomplished without sacrifice.

WHAT ARE YOU WILLING TO SACRIFICE TO BECOME MORE LIKE THE SAVIOR?

TALK ABOUT IT!

1. Why does God ask us to be willing to give up what we love most? Doesn't He want us to be happy?

2. Does something you had to sacrifice for mean more than something you didn't? Why do you think that is?

3. Oftentimes, our sacrifices are giving up things that are immediate (like money, time or comfort) for things that are in the future (happiness, future fulfillment, a place in heaven). It can be difficult to give up immediate happiness for joy in the future. What can you do to help remind yourself of what matters most?

CLARA BARTON: CIVIL WAR NURSE

"You must never so much as think whether you like it or not; whether it is bearable or not; You must never think of anything except the need and how to meet it."

—Clara Barton

CLARISSA HARLOWE BARTON, OR CLARA, AS SHE WAS CALLED, WAS born on Christmas day in 1821. She grew up in Massachusetts, the daughter of a well-to-do businessman. Her life of service and sacrifice began at a young age. When Clara was just eleven years old, her elder brother, David, was badly injured in a fall. Clara gave up her time and schooling for two years to stay by his bedside and help nurse him back to health.

When the American Civil War broke out in 1861, Clara was anxious to help. She told a friend that she felt guilty for having so much and being so safe while the soldiers were living with so little and risking their lives for her. So, she took it upon herself to gather supplies for the soldiers, providing as much as she could from her own resources of money, food, and clothing. There are many stories of hungry, sick, and discouraged soldiers looking up and seeing Clara driving up with a wagon full of much needed supplies.

In addition to providing supplies, Clara assisted the army surgeons with operations and directly cared for wounded soldiers left on the battlefields. At the battle of Fredericksburg, she didn't even wait for the battle to end before she began treating the injured soldiers. With bullets flying around her, Clara did all she could to help and comfort the wounded and dying men. In gratitude, they nicknamed her the "Angel of the Battlefield."

After the war, Clara saw that many families were anxious for news of their sons, husbands, and brothers who went missing during the war. Once again, Clara stepped in to fill that need. She started the Missing Soldiers Office on the third floor of her boardinghouse and was immediately flooded with letters asking her to help locate their loved ones. Initially, Clara was using her own money and resources to run the office, but it became clear that she would need more help and more money than she had, so she went on speaking tours to help cover the costs. When the office closed in 1868 Clara and her team had helped find the whereabouts of over 22,000 missing soldiers, bringing comfort and closure to thousands of grieving families.

When this service was complete, Clara traveled to Europe for some much-needed rest. While there, she was introduced to the International Red Cross, which was founded to help the sick and wounded during times of war, and to give volunteer aid to all who needed it, regardless of their country or which political side they were on. Clara was inspired and returned home determined to start the American chapter of the Red Cross. She served as its president for over 30 years, until she finally retired at the age of 83.

Clara Barton could have lived a life of ease and comfort, but she chose instead to give her money, health, food and time to those whose lives were harder than her own. Never content to simply watch people struggle, Clara did all she could and gave all she had to comfort those around her.

> If anyone desires to come after Me, he must deny himself, and take up his cross daily, and follow Me.
>
> For whoever desires to save his life will lose it, but whoever loses his life for My sake will save it.
>
> —Luke 9:23–24 (NKJV)

TRY IT!

Think of the goals and desires you have for your life. Ask yourself the following questions:

- What am I willing to sacrifice to achieve these goals?

- If God asks, would I be willing to give these things up for Him?

- Do I have enough faith to believe that when I sacrifice my desires to His, He will bless me with something even better?

9. STRONG SUPPORTS

During the coldest months of the year, penguins in the Arctic will huddle up in a group to keep warm. The penguins on the outside of the huddle take the full force of the driving wind and snow, in order to shelter the penguins in the middle. Then, after a time, all of the penguins suddenly shift spots. Now the penguins who were nice and warm from being in the middle take their turn on the outside, and the ones who were out in the cold, get their turn to be warmed by the group in the middle. All throughout the cold, dark winter they take turns protecting and being protected.

There have been many times in my life when people have told me things like, "I really loved your theater production. It is so nice to have something good and uplift-

> One of the greatest gifts you can give another person is the gift of your support.

ing to take my family to. I can't wait for you to do another one!" Then, later on, when I was ready to do another production and was asking people for financial backing, labor or help of any kind, these same people have told me that they are unable to help. I found myself getting frustrated. So many people wanted the good things I was trying to put out there, but so many of them weren't willing to actually support the effort required to bring them about.

However, the more I thought about it, the more I realized I am guilty of the same thing. How many times have I been grateful for an uplifting movie and then borrowed it from a friend instead of paying to buy it myself? How many times have I seen beautiful and inspiring pieces of art and failed to support the artist? How many times do I see a worthy cause and convince myself that I don't have enough money or time to contribute?

The penguins don't get all warm in the middle of the huddle and then refuse to take their turn on the outside. Everyone takes their turn in the wind and cold. Only by working together are they able to be truly effective.

At times it may be our turn to stand at the front of a particular cause, challenge or project. We may be the ones in the center of the huddle, relying on the strength and help of those around us. At other times, it may be our turn to be the support; the ones taking the full brunt of the storm; the ones that help bear the weight and hold up the people fighting on our behalf. We are on this earth together, not by accident, but because we need one another. We literally cannot make it to Heaven alone. Because just like the penguin huddle, life is a group effort.

We rise higher by lifting others.

FROM THE BIBLE: HELPING MOSES

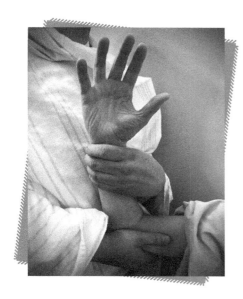

For even the Son of man came not to be ministered unto, but to minister, and to give his life a ransom for many.

—Mark 10:45

IN THE BOOK OF EXODUS, WE read of a time when the Israelites were fighting against the army of the Amalekites. As they fought, Moses went up onto a hill with Aaron and Hur. When Moses held up his hands, the Israelite army began to win, but when he lowered his hands, the Amalekite army began winning instead.

Moses held up his arms for as long as he could so the Israelites would defeat the Amalekites, but his arms quickly became heavy and ached so much that he could no longer keep them raised by himself. Aaron and Hur saw this and quickly helped Moses sit on a nearby rock. Then Aaron stood on one side and Hur stood on the other, each holding up one of Moses' arms. In this way, Moses was able to keep his arms up the entire day until the battle was finally won (Exodus 17:8–13).

Sometimes we think playing a supportive role means that we are less important or needed than the ones we think are doing the "actual work." For instance, we can look at this story and say that Aaron and Hur were less important than Moses, because they couldn't raise their arms and change the battle. Or we can look at their efforts and acknowledge that even though it was Moses who had the power to give victory to the Israelites, he simply could not have done it without their help.

The word support means to hold up or bear the weight of some-thing. It's easy to see that a bridge would collapse if we suddenly took away its support beams; that Israel would have lost without Aaron and Hur; that a basketball team with only one player won't win, no matter how good that player is. It doesn't matter whether we are taking our turn as the star player or as a member of the support team, because we are all important. A true support is not something that's unnecessary, or simply nice to have—it is essential!

TALK ABOUT IT!

1. Why do you think the Lord didn't just bless Moses to be able to keep his arms up without help?

2. Why do you think we feel like supporting roles aren't as important as the main role?

3. What are some things you can do to support the righteous efforts of the people around you?

SALVATION ARMY: DOUGHNUT LASSIES

"There was a prayer in my heart that somehow this home touch would do more for those who ate the doughnuts than satisfy a physical hunger."

—Helen Purviance

IN APRIL 1917, WHEN AMERICA ENTERED WORLD WAR I, THE Salvation Army immediately looked for ways they could support the soldiers who were fighting on the front. Evangeline Booth, the National Commander for the Salvation Army, sent eleven young ladies to France to support and uplift the soldiers there. They set up rest stations, hostels and support huts wherever the soldiers were fighting—some of them right on the front lines, where they were in danger of bombshells and poisonous mustard gas.

By October there were many more Salvation Army officers stationed in France. Ensigns Helen Purviance and Margaret Sheldon were two of them. When they saw the despair and homesickness of the soldiers, these two young women decided to do what they could to lift the soldier's spirits with a special treat from home.

They had flour, sugar, lard, baking powder, and cinnamon, so they decided to make doughnuts. They had to shape them by hand and could only fry seven at a time in the one small pan they had. The smell of frying doughnuts quickly began to spread through the camp and the soldiers stood eagerly in the rain to get their doughnuts. That first day, though the two women worked into the night, they were only able to make 150 doughnuts. The next day, that number doubled, and when they received more equipment and help, they were making up to 9,000 doughnuts!

Can you imagine what that seemingly small gesture meant to those tired, cold, homesick, struggling soldiers? How it gave them hope and comfort and the strength to keep fighting?

You may not think your contribution is important or that it will amount to much. When you find yourself thinking those thoughts, remind yourself that a few doughnuts in the face of World War I probably didn't seem like much either. Then go out and support the things, the people and the causes you are passionate about in any way you can!

TRY IT!

- Make a list of some of the people, organizations, or causes you would like to support.

- Then make a list of the ways you can support them in ways big and small!

- Pick one thing you can do now and get started right away!

A PORTRAIT IN COURAGE:
ANDRÉE DE JONGH

"When war was declared I knew what needed to be done. There was no hesitation. We could not stop what we had to do although we knew the cost. Even if it was at the expense of our lives, we had to fight until the last breath."

—Andrée de Jongh

ANDRÉE DE JONGH (1916–2007): *Andrée began her resistance work in 1940, as soon as the Germans advanced into Belgium. She began helping Allied soldiers who were injured or trapped behind enemy lines, by taking them to safe houses. She soon realized the need to get them out of Belgium altogether, so she started an escape route called the Comet Line that took the men from Belgium, through occupied France, and all the way into Spain. Andrée made around twenty trips, all on foot, escorting over one hundred men to freedom. She was captured by the Germans in 1943 and sent to Ravensbrück Concentration camp for the rest of the war, until she was freed by the Allies in 1945. By the end of the war, the Comet Line that she started, had helped bring over seven hundred soldiers to safety.*

SECTION 3:

WEAPONS TRAINING

The most powerful weapons in the world won't do you any good if you don't know how to use them.

10. CRACKING THE ENEMY'S CODE

During World War II, radio signals in Morse code were often used for communication within the armies on both sides. Because radio signals could be easily intercepted, they began encoding the messages with increasingly complicated codes and ciphers. However, cryptologists frequently broke the codes and were able to read the messages anyway.

But then suddenly, all that changed. The Germans had begun using a special machine that could produce thousands of different cipher codes. It was called the Enigma machine, and the codes it produced were said to be unbreakable. All of a sudden the British code breakers could not read any of the German communications. At the time, the biggest threat was the German U-boats in the Atlantic Ocean. They were constantly sinking the allied supply ships, and because the allies couldn't read the German messages, they had no way of knowing where the U-boats were going to be at any given time.

British cryptologists were working around the clock to find a way to break the Enigma's codes, but the code changed every day, and with 150 million, million, million possible combinations for each message, the task seemed impossible! The Allies built a machine that could help break the codes, but it took so long to decipher the messages that by the time they knew what the message was, the information in it was no longer relevant. At last, they realized that every day the German communications would send a weather report and that most messages ended with "Heil Hitler!" Knowing the words "weather" and "Heil Hitler" were in each message helped them figure out the key and to once again read the German messages.

They were able to find out where the U-boats would be, and then alert their supply ships, so they could avoid them. The much-needed supplies were able to reach Europe, and the Allies were also able to decode other intercepted communications giving them advanced knowledge of German tactics. It has been estimated that the cracking of the Enigma codes shortened the war by about two years, saving millions of lives!

In a war there is obviously a huge advantage to knowing the enemy's plans ahead of time. If you know where and when he will attack, you can fortify the spot. If you know what weapons and tactics he will use, you can know which defenses to prepare. We are in a war now—a war against evil and Satan, the father of all lies. And it is just as vital for us to know his tactics so we can be prepared and better protected.

FROM THE BIBLE: THE FATHER OF ALL LIES

He was a murderer from the beginning, and abode not in the truth, because there is no truth in him. When he speaketh a lie, he speaketh of his own: for he is a liar, and the father of it.

—John 8:44

JUST LIKE THE CRYPTOLO-gists who were able to crack the code of their enemies, we have the ability to decode the tactics of Satan. With holy scripture, we have been given the perfect codebook for deciphering Satan's plan in this spiritual war.

The book of Revelation gives us an important key: "And the great dragon was cast out, that old serpent, called the Devil, and Satan, which deceiveth the whole world: he was cast out into the earth, and his angels were cast out with him. . . . Woe to the inhabiters of the earth and of the sea! for the devil has come down unto you, having great wrath, because he knoweth that he hath but a short time" (Revelation 12:9, 12).

In 2 Corinthians 4:4 it says that Satan "hath blinded the minds of them which believe not, lest the light of the glorious gospel of Christ, who is the image of God, should shine unto them."

Acts 13:10 describes Satan like this: "O full of all subtlety and all mischief . . . thou enemy of all righteousness, wilt thou not cease to pervert the right ways of the Lord?"

These verses show us someone who is extremely angry! They show us someone who lies and deceives, and someone who is willing to do whatever he can to get what he wants. Satan is angry because you have what he never will. You have a body, life on this earth, opportunities to grow, love, joy, and light. He is incredibly jealous and will do anything he can to destroy your happiness and the peace you find in Christ. In short, his goal is to make you as miserable as he is!

So we know his goal is to make us miserable, but how does he plan on doing that? Following are some of his most frequently used tactics. As you read through these, be prayerful and open to which of these weapons Satan tends to use on you the most.

WEAPONS OF THE ENEMY:

DISCOURAGEMENT

One of Satan's most powerful tools is discouragement. He is really good at making things seem hopeless and pointless. He is the one whispering to you that what you do doesn't really matter; that your efforts are too pitiful and lame to accomplish anything; that no one is listening anyway; and that you aren't smart enough, brave enough, important enough, or talented enough to make a difference.

He knows that if you feel like it's hopeless, you will stop trying to make a difference. He won't need to worry about stopping you anymore, because you will have stopped yourself.

Discouragement is so powerful and sneaky because it doesn't necessarily make us stop believing in God. But it does stop us from turning to Him. It takes away our hope, saps our energy and drains our motivation. It makes us say, "Why should I even try. It won't make a difference anyway."

TALK ABOUT IT!

1. Have you ever felt truly discouraged? What helped you out of it?

2. What are some things you can do to stay positive when things get hard?

FEAR

Another one of Satan's tactics is fear. He loves it when we are full of fear. He loves it not only because it makes us unhappy but because he knows that when we are full of fear we cannot also be full of faith. When we are full of fear we have no room to acknowledge that God is in charge and that we are in His hands.

Remember Peter, who was able to walk on the water as long as he kept his eyes on the Savior? When he looked away from the Savior and focused on the storm around him he became afraid and began to sink. (Matthew 14:22–33) We can't focus on the Savior and on the storm at the same time.

Once again, Satan doesn't need us to stop believing in God and Jesus Christ, he simply needs us to take our eyes off them and focus on the storms around us. He knows that if we are fearful, he can stop us from accomplishing good things.

Through fear he can stop us from opening our mouths and sharing truth. Through fear he can stop us from developing and using our talents. Through fear he can stop us from loving one another. And through fear he can stop us from becoming the joyful, powerful beings that even he knows we can become.

TALK ABOUT IT!

1. What are some of the fears holding you back from doing what you truly want?

2. How can you focus on the Savior instead of your fears?

DISTRACTION

Sometimes we have every intention of doing good, serving others, or starting a new project or habit that we know will make a difference. However, life gets busy, and we can get distracted by all the things around us. That TV show everyone else is watching, the alerts on our phones, the abundance of opportunities available to us and the constant flow of information and noise can all distract us.

Whenever my dog wants something, like the bacon in my hand, for example, he will sit and stare at that piece of bacon with incredible laser focus! All kinds of other things can be going on around him, but he will stay focused on that bacon in my hand. I can even get up and move, and he will move along with me without taking his eyes off the bacon. We can't even distract him with his usual dog food or treats. He wants the bacon because he recognizes it as a superior prize!

> Be sober, be vigilant; because your adversary the devil, as a roaring lion, walketh about, seeking whom he may devour.
>
> —1 Peter 5:8

In this life there is so much to distract us. These are not necessarily bad things. There is nothing wrong with watching good TV shows or checking our phones or participating in fun activities. They only become a problem when they take us away from what is truly important. It's pretty easy to see how the negative things in our lives stop us from getting what we want. However, it can be much more difficult to notice when good things keep us from the most important and worthwhile things. Don't let the good things distract you from the best things. In other words: Focus on the bacon!

TALK ABOUT IT!

1. What are the most important things in your life?

2. When you reach the end of your life, what do you want to have accomplished?

3. What are some things that may be distracting you from these goals, and what can you do today to remove them?

PROPAGANDA

There is a whole lot of information out there. We have information at our fingertips twenty-four hours a day, seven days a week. We hear it everywhere we go. It appears on our screens, whether we look it up or not. We are constantly being fed information. However, it is important to remember that information is not the same as truth.

During wartime, governments often use propaganda to influence and manipulate the people. For example, during World War II Hitler and the Nazis used propaganda techniques to make the Germans think that Jews were second-class citizens, that pure Germans were a superior race, and that the people in the countries they conquered were happy to have them there! It seems incredible looking back that people would believe those things. And yet, they did.

You may not be aware of how frequently you, too, are hearing propaganda today that is just as false. Propaganda likes to use words and phrases that make people react in an emotional way. "Love" and "hate" are two such words. Propaganda also likes to make you feel that there are only two options, and that if you don't believe what they are telling you, you must be bigoted, evil, or stupid. But that is not true. You can disagree with someone and still be smart, still be good, and still be non-judgmental.

There are so many ways Satan twists information to his purposes. Propaganda is powerful, and we must learn to recognize when we are hearing it so we can make our own decisions about what we believe.

TALK ABOUT IT!

1. What trusted resources do you have that can help you know what is true and what isn't?

2. How can you be more selective about the information you choose to take in?

COUNTERFEITS

One of the devil's favorite weapons is the use of counterfeits. Now, it's important to remember that a counterfeit is not the opposite of something good—it is a twisted version of it. Counterfeit money, for instance, is not the opposite of money, it is fake money. On a more spiritual level, love is the beautiful truth given us from God, but lust is its counterfeit. Faith is a real power linking us to Heavenly Father. Superstition or faith in things that are not true is the counterfeit.

On the surface the truth and its counterfeit may be easily confused, but when you look closely you will see that they lead to different outcomes. Real faith will bring you closer to your Father in Heaven, but superstition will lead you to fear. Real love will help you be more selfless, patient and kind, but the counterfeit is all about satisfying yourself.

Practice recognizing the counterfeits around you, always praying and asking for the Holy Spirit to help you.

HALF-TRUTHS

Half-truths are another tool of the devil. For instance, the commandment to love your neighbor as yourself is one that seems pretty clear-cut. Jesus taught in the New Testament that everyone is our neighbor and that we should have love and compassion for everyone. Now, Satan knows that he can't convince us that loving others is wrong. It's pretty obvious that love is a great and holy thing. So instead of trying to convince us that it's wrong to love others, he tries to convince us that we should love everyone—except for the people who hurt others. He makes it seem natural that we don't need to love people like Hitler, Osama Bin Laden, members of the Ku Klux Klan, or anyone else who does unspeakable evil. But is that what Jesus taught, that we must love everyone—except for those we don't think are worthy? Is it okay to be tolerant of everyone's beliefs, except for the people who are intolerant of our beliefs? No. When Jesus commanded us to love our neighbor, He meant everyone. Truth is powerful, whole, and complete and never changing. Don't settle for only half of it.

CONTENTION

Have you ever been in an argument where both sides end up hurt and angry? It probably happens quite a lot. In fact, when we argue, the result is usually anger and hurt feelings with neither side changing their mind. We usually start out with good intentions when we are debating a point. We know that our knowledge can help them or bring them peace. However, sometimes we get so focused on convincing the other side that we are right and they are wrong that we become frustrated and angry. And then no one feels peaceful. Satan loves this because he knows that it doesn't really matter which side is right, if he can get both sides angry and hurt. And when that happens, both sides lose.

Have you heard the phrase "divide and conquer"? It was first used in Roman times to describe a military and political strategy where the ruling side would not allow their various enemies to unite. They knew that if they could keep the people divided, they wouldn't band together and overthrow those trying to control them.

Satan wants to divide us from one another for the same reason. He wants us to be separated by our differences. He wants us to fight. He wants us to feel angry and annoyed with one another. He wants us to feel alone and isolated so we don't tap into the power of working together. He wants us to be more concerned with being right than being kind. He wants us to be so hung up on our differences that we can't join forces with each other. He wants to divide and conquer!

TRY IT!

- There is power and strength in unity, which is why the enemy tries so hard to stop us from working together. What is one thing you can do to be more united with the people around you?

- Next time you find yourself arguing a point with someone, stop and ask yourself: Would I rather be right, or would I rather be happy?

LAZINESS & APATHY

Apathy is not caring or being interested in the world and people around you. It is failing to stand up for what's right because it seems pointless. It is refusing to try because something seems too hard. It is assuming and/or hoping that someone else will take care of the problem. Apathy's close cousins are laziness, selfishness, and cynicism.

Sometimes we fall into apathy because we know that once we recognize a need, we have an obligation to help fill that need, and we don't want to accept the responsibility that comes with caring. Sometimes we fall into apathy because we don't take the time to find out what is really going on in the world around us. Sometimes our apathy comes out of fear and selfishness. But in the end it doesn't matter where our apathy comes from if it stops us from caring and participating in the world around us.

Remember, the devil is happy if he can get us to do bad things, but he is just as satisfied if he can merely stop us from doing good things. If he can get us to sit on the sidelines instead of participate, he has won. We are responsible for the things we do, and for the things we do not do. In the end it doesn't matter what we believe if we don't act on it.

TEMPTATIONS & JUSTIFICATION

One of Satan's greatest tools is the way he gets inside our minds and tries to use our weaknesses against us. He always seems to tempt us in exactly the ways it is most difficult for us to resist. He tells us that our choices won't affect anyone but us. He tells us that what we're doing isn't as bad as what other people are doing, so we must be okay. He tells us that if we don't go along with what everyone else is doing, we'll be alone. He tells us that wickedness and selfishness will make us happy. He convinces us that it's okay to do a little wrong, because we can always repent later, and no harm will be done. He makes evil looks so tempting, easy and acceptable. But here's the thing, he has no power to deliver on his promises. He doesn't actually care if you are happy or accepted. He will simply tell you anything in order to get you to make the choice he wants for you.

> **The world will not be destroyed by those who do evil, but by those who watch them without doing anything.**
>
> **—Albert Einstein**

TALK ABOUT IT!

1. Have you ever found yourself thinking, "Well, I might not be making the best choice here, but it's a lot better than what other people are doing, so I'm still okay." What is so dangerous about this way of thinking?

2. Can we accurately gauge our righteousness by comparing ourselves to others? How can you accurately gauge how you are doing?

A FALSE SENSE OF SECURITY

I have a friend who loves snakes. She feeds her pet snakes live mice. When she first puts the mouse in with a snake, the mouse, recognizing the snake as a threat, frantically runs and runs, trying to get out of the cage. But the snake just lies there, completely still. It doesn't strike, or even seem to notice the mouse at all.

After a while, the mouse starts to slow down, but it keeps on high alert. It watches the snake, ready to dart away if the snake looks like it's about to strike. But still the snake doesn't move. Finally, the mouse, no longer believing that the snake is a danger, stops moving. It is then that the snake strikes and the mouse is eaten.

The mouse was eaten because it stopped seeing the snake as a threat. The mouse thought the snake would immediately attack and when it just sat there doing nothing, the mouse was confused, assumed it had misjudged the snake, and stopped running. It is a mistake to assume that if we don't see immediate negative consequences for our actions, they are spiritually safe. Sometimes we may not see the consequences for a long time, but they are real and they will catch up with us—often in ways that we aren't expecting.

TALK ABOUT IT!

• How does Satan try to convince you that he's not a threat, and that the things he wants you to do aren't going to harm you?

THROWING OUT THE BABY WITH THE BATH WATER

Have you heard the phrase, "don't throw out the baby with the bath water"? It means don't accidentally throw out what is good, when you are throwing out the bad. One of the tactics the devil likes to use is the false idea that just because someone has done something which we feel is bad, it cancels out all the good they have done. For example, ignoring all the good done by America's founding fathers, just because some of them had slaves. Or condemning other historical figures because some of the things they said are culturally insensitive by today's standards. Or perhaps, not listening to church leaders or other people of faith because we have seen some mistakes they have made.

But here's the thing: None of us are perfect. The only perfect being to ever be on the earth was Jesus Christ. We all make mistakes and bad choices throughout our lives, but thankfully God doesn't discount all the good we are trying to do because of those mistakes. Remember that we are all imperfect people who are just doing our best and light and truth is still light and truth, whether the person sharing it is perfect or not. Don't ignore the good around you just because it came from an imperfect source. Don't throw the baby out with the bath water.

TALK ABOUT IT!

1. Can you recognize times where any of these weapons have been used against you?

2. How can knowing what these tactics are help you avoid them in the future?

INCENDIARY BOMBS: THE BOMBING OF ST. PAUL'S

"Glares of many fires and sweeping clouds of smoke kept hiding the shape. Suddenly, the shining cross, dome and towers stood out like a symbol in the inferno."

—Herbert Mason

DURING WORLD WAR II THE GERMANS REPEATEDLY BOMBED London in what would become known as the Blitz. More than 30,000 tons of bombs were dropped on the city from September 1940 to May 1941. After a few months, much of London lay in ruins.

On the night of December 29th, the bombing, which had briefly stopped for Christmas, began again. When the bombs began to fall around St. Paul's Cathedral, a group of volunteers rushed to save that sacred and historic landmark.

The bombers were using a special kind of device called an incendiary bomb. Instead of blowing up whatever it hit, these bombs were designed to start a fire that would then spread throughout the buildings. It started small, but the fire would quickly rage out of control. The volunteers spent all night racing up, down, and around the cathedral, wherever the bombs fell, so they could put out the fires. The bombing was relentless, but the volunteers continued putting them out, one after another.

The next morning, as dawn broke over London a scene of devastation was seen on all sides. But from the smoke and piles of rubble rose the unharmed dome of St. Paul's.

TALK ABOUT IT

1. Incendiary bombs might seem less harmful than a regular bomb, because they don't explode, but what do you think can make them more dangerous? What kind of subtle or seemingly less harmful devices does Satan try to use on you?

2. Do you ever find yourself focusing on the "big" sins, and not worrying so much about the "little" sins? What does this story help you learn about that?

3. What can you learn from the way the volunteers responded to these bombs?

11. PREPARING FOR THE ATTACK

Have you ever participated in a one-time self-defense class where you learn some really cool and effective techniques for fighting off an attacker? During the class, you think, "Wow, this is great stuff. I am definitely going to use this if I ever get attacked." Now, imagine that several months, or even years, go by and you never once have the need to use the techniques that you learned. Then, suddenly, one day, you are attacked. Your brain flies into panic mode. Your heart is racing, the adrenaline is pumping, and then . . . you freeze!

Are you suddenly able to execute the technique with the speed and confidence needed to make it effective? No. At this point, you'll be lucky to even remember what the technique was.

The reason for this is that it takes twice as long for the danger signals to reach the decision making part of your brain as it does the panic part of your brain. So you panic and then freeze. The way to overcome this is to practice your response so that it becomes instinctive. In other words, you're able to react without waiting for the frontal lobe of your brain to kick in and decide what to do.

For your spiritual self-defense to be effective, the same rules apply. You must decide ahead of time what to do or say and then you need to practice it until it becomes instinctive. Benjamin Franklin said, "By failing to prepare, you are preparing to fail." In the moment when we are being tempted, it can be hard to think clearly because our emotions and fears are so involved. By planning ahead, you can be prepared and respond to the situation with calm confidence instead of reacting in a panic.

CONFIDENCE COMES FROM BEING PREPARED.

TALK ABOUT IT!

1. What are some things you are frequently tempted by?

2. How can you plan ahead to be better prepared to face them?

3. What are some ways you and your friends or family can help one another be better prepared to face temptation?

FROM THE BIBLE: THE ARMOR OF GOD

Finally my brethren, be strong in the Lord and in the power of His might. Put on the whole armour of God, that ye may be able to stand against the wiles of the devil. For we wrestle not against flesh and blood, but against principalities, against powers, against the rulers of the darkness of this world, against spiritual wickedness in high places.

—Ephesians 6:10–12

NOTICE IN THE ABOVE SCRIPTURE THAT WE ARE TOLD TO PUT ON THE WHOLE armor of God, not just part of it. Obviously it's not enough to simply put on a helmet, and leave off the breastplate, or to swing a sword without holding the shield. The same goes for our spiritual armor. The truth and knowledge we have doesn't do much if we don't use it and share it. We must be prepared, and in order to effectively use the power of the word of God, we must know what His word is. Similarly, it's not enough to merely say we have faith; we have to act on it. And only occasionally making righteous choices isn't enough either. We must persevere in righteousness and faith until the end of the fight.

Following are some specific weapons you can use in your fight against the enemy. Remember that, just like with physical weapons, learning to wield most spiritual weapons successfully also takes learning and practice. But if you prepare and strive to do your best, God will be with you and work through you to defeat the enemy in whatever form it comes.

YOUR WEAPONS:

PRAYER

Did you know that you have access to the most powerful being in the universe whenever you want? Prayer is one of the most powerful weapons we have against the enemy. It's incredible to think that through prayer, you can get help and comfort from the ultimate source of guidance, strength, and comfort!

When you are tempted to say something unkind, watch a movie you know is inappropriate, or go to that party you know you shouldn't attend, stop for a moment and pray. It doesn't need to be a big production. You don't need to kneel down and say a prayer out loud while everyone looks on. You can just say a quick prayer in your mind, wherever you happen to be at the moment, asking for the strength and courage to resist temptation. I promise you it will help!

Prayer can be a powerful weapon in other ways as well. Often, when we are feeling upset or need advice or comfort, we turn to the people around us. But have you ever tried turning to Heavenly Father first? I have found that when I pray to Him first, I am much more at peace, and my mind is much clearer, even if I do ask someone else for help as well. Prayer helps me have the peace and inspiration to seek out the best person for the help I need. It helps me say things in the right way and not say something I will regret later. In short, it helps me be open to the help and the answers I need.

You are not here to face all the trials and temptations of life alone. Your loving Heavenly Father knows that you will need help, and He is there, ready to shower you with comfort and strength and guidance. So don't forget to ask!

TRY IT!

- Next time you are tempted or feel the need to vent, try seeking advice or comfort from God through prayer first before turning to someone else.

GOSPEL KNOWLEDGE

You couldn't be a doctor without knowing how to heal. You couldn't become a lawyer without studying the law. So how can you expect to be a disciple of Jesus Christ if you don't know what He taught, and haven't practiced living as a follower of Christ would?

We have so much information at our fingertips today. We have access to history, scriptures, and religious teachings like no one has ever had before, but that information will not do us any good if we don't study it. We have to know what we believe in order to live it, in order to teach it, and in order to defend it. In the past it may have been possible to skate by on a surface amount of gospel knowledge, but those times are long gone.

A tree needs deep roots to withstand a storm. The stronger the wind, the deeper those roosts must be. We have information like we never have before, but Satan is getting more and more angry and desperate to tear us down. In order to withstand the mighty winds, we must grow the deepest roots we can; we must learn and live the word of God like never before.

JESUS: YOUR MOST POWERFUL ALLY

Jesus is the Light. The closer we get to Him, the more clearly His light helps us see and recognize the dangers around us. His light makes it easier to recognize the lies of Satan, and easier to draw on the Lord's power and comfort in our lives.

So how do we draw closer to the Savior? Well, how would you get closer to someone you met? You would talk with them and spend time with them. You would want to know all about them: their interests, what they liked, what they believed. You would

> Draw near to God and He will draw near to you.
>
> —James 4:8 (NKJV)

also want your new friend to know about you. You would want to confide in them and turn to them for support and advice.

Getting close to someone is a two-way job. You both have to share and truly listen in return. Jesus is already the perfect friend. He knows you better than you know yourself. He loves to hear from you about every little thing going on in your life. And He is always there to listen and to help you in any way He can. However, if you want to truly know the Savior, you have to do your part too. Study His life, read His words, practice His teachings, and, of course, talk to Him. Not just in formal prayer, but in your heart throughout the day. You are never alone with the Savior by your side.

TRY IT!

- Today when you pray, try to visualize your Father in Heaven and the Savior listening to you. Tell them about your day, about your hopes and fears. Be honest. Don't worry about using heightened "prayer language." Just talk.

- After you are finished talking, listen. Don't be afraid of silence. Remain still and listen to any thoughts or feelings that come to you.

COMMANDING SATAN TO DEPART

In 1 Peter 5:8 we are told that Satan goes about as a roaring lion, seeking whom he can devour. He is angry and bitter and wants us to suffer just like he does. We may not see him, but he comes to us in the negative, mean, and hurtful thoughts we think about ourselves and others. He comes to us in the temptations we feel to do things we know are not right.

Sometimes, it seems that no matter how much we are trying to do good, Satan will not leave us alone. In the New Testament we read of the temptation of Christ, when Satan appeared to the Savior as he was about to start his ministry and tempted him to use his power improperly. We can learn a great lesson from how the Savior reacted to him. The Bible says, "Then saith Jesus unto him, Get thee hence, Satan. . . Then the devil leaveth him, and, behold, angels came and ministered unto him." (Matt. 4:10–11) When tempted, the Lord simply commanded Satan to leave him, and Satan had to go.

Did you know that through the power of Jesus Christ, you can do the same thing? You, too, can command the devil to depart, and

SECTION 3: WEAPONS TRAINING

because God's power is stronger than Satan's he will have to leave you alone.

TRY IT!

• Next time you are feeling tempted, or negative thoughts are crowding in and threatening to bring you down, say a prayer and, in the name of Jesus Christ, command Satan to leave. The power of Jesus Christ will force Satan to retreat.

THE GIFT OF DISCERNMENT

When you are being constantly bombarded with lies, it can become difficult not to believe them. They can seem so plausible and make so much sense in our minds. Satan is so good at taking truth and twisting it, and at making things that are completely false seem true. People, organizations, products and media of all kinds seem to be constantly fighting to convince us that what they say is true, and that everyone else is wrong. So how can you tell the difference? How do you know who and what to believe?

During the Gold Rush, many inexperienced people who were panning for gold became excited when they found shiny, gold pieces in their pans. What they found looked like gold on the outside, but when they took it to be tested it became apparent that it was not gold. It was a substance called pyrite. Pyrite became known as fool's gold because it tricked so many people. However, if you know what to look for, and what tests to perform, it can be quite easy to tell the difference between real gold and fool's gold because,

> But the natural man receiveth not the things of the Spirit of God: for they are foolishness to him: neither can he know them, because they are spiritually discerned.
>
> —1 Corinthians 2:14

in spite of their similar color, they actually have quite a different makeup.

The apostle Matthew warns us that in these last days there will be many "false Christs and false prophets" who will try to deceive us. (Matthew 24:24) You can learn to tell the difference between the truth and the fool's gold of Satan's philosophies and promises. In fact, we are told not just to take things at face value and to assume that something is good and right just because people tell us it is. We are told to "Prove all things; hold fast that which is good." (1 Thessalonians 5:21)

So what are some of the tests we can apply? We can remember that spiritual knowledge comes from spiritual sources. We must use our minds, of course, but spiritual things must also be learned through the Spirit. Faith can't be understood only by the intellect; it must be felt and understood through the Spirit as well. In other words, we must use our minds and our hearts or spirits to know what is true.

One of the quickest and easiest ways to tell the difference between gold and fool's gold is to have a sample of each and compare them to each other. You can do the same with things of the Spirit. The more familiar you are with the gold of Jesus' teachings, the more easily you will be able to tell the difference between those teachings and Satan's counterfeits and lies. The more you feel the peace that comes with following the Lord, the easier it will be to recognize the confusion of the adversary. Remember, the more you surround yourself with the real deal, the less likely you are to be deceived by what is fake.

> And be not conformed to this world: but be ye transformed by the renewing of your mind, that ye may prove what is that good, and acceptable, and perfect, will of God.
>
> —Romans 12:2

ASK YOURSELF:

1. Does what I'm hearing make sense in my mind and in my heart?

2. Does it follow the teachings of the Savior?

3. Have I prayed for guidance about this subject? What did I feel concerning it?

4. Does this message bring peace or confusion?

5. Am I doing all I can to stay close to my Father in Heaven, so I won't be deceived?

THE POWER OF HOPE

Several times I have been on an airplane when the weather on the ground was gray and rainy. Then, when the plane took off and broke through the clouds, the gray and rain was instantly gone and the sun was suddenly shining brightly. Growing up in a place where it was overcast and rainy for a large portion of the year, I always found it comforting to know that even when I couldn't see it, the sun was always there on the other side of the clouds.

Hope is believing that there is sunshine on the other side of the clouds; that there is light, even amidst the darkness. Satan wants you to believe that the darkness is all that exists, that things are hopeless, and that we have every reason to be discouraged or give up. But light is stronger than darkness! Where there is light, darkness cannot exist because light literally drives away the darkness. Fill your soul and your life with the light of Christ. Do all you can to invite the light of Christ into your life. Live in a way that the Spirit of God can shine through you!

> Hope begins in the dark, the stubborn hope that if you just show up and try to do the right thing, the dawn will come. You wait and watch and work: You don't give up.
>
> —Anne Lamott

Hope doesn't take away all the darkness and difficulty. It doesn't mean that you won't have to walk through the darkness. It means you can walk through the darkness, with hope that there is light at the other end. It means you can face discouragement and evil, confident in the fact that through Christ you have the power to overcome it. Hope is believing while the earth is covered in snow, that spring will come again. It is believing that all the hard things we are going through in this life have a purpose. It is believing that ultimately all darkness will be gone, that all evil will be overcome, and that all wrongs will be made right.

Now the God of hope fill you with all joy and peace
in believing, that ye may abound in hope through the
power of the Holy Ghost.

—Romans 15:13

REFLECTING GOD'S LIGHT
In the days of wooden sailing ships, fire on board was extremely dangerous. Because lanterns and candles could so easily tip over and burn down the ship, they came up with a clever way to bring light below decks. They placed a prism in the deck of the ship that would sit flush with the planking, but would hang down into the rooms below. From up above, it looked like a glass tile in the middle of the decking, and from below it looked like a light fixture on the ceiling. When the sun shined down on the top deck, it traveled through the prism and was refracted into the decks below. In this way, the sun could reach into the darkness it otherwise could not penetrate.

Every tiny bit of light we send out in the world dispels a bit of darkness. Every time we smile at a stranger; every time we share the truth; every time we pray or create something of beauty; every time we help someone; every time we act in faith, we are dispelling the darkness with light.

Like the deck prisms, we are not the source of light and truth. It is the Lord's light—His power—that converts, comforts, and heals. We do not need to have all the answers, because God does. We do not need to be all powerful, because He is. Our job is simply to be the instrument through which the Lord can do His miracles. If we keep ourselves clean and ready, the Lord will use us to shine light into the darkest of places.

FILLING THE HOLE
Have you ever tried to dig a hole in the sand? The sand tends to slide back into the hole almost as fast as you can dig. Even a hole dug in the dirt will fill back in overtime as the wind blows dirt and debris into the opening. But what happens if you immediately fill that hole with something else, like mineral rich potting soil and a seed? Not only does the plant stop the hole from refilling with debris, it also produces something beautiful and worthwhile.

When we only focus on removing the bad influences from our lives, the same thing can happen. It is not enough to simply remove the bad from the world and our lives, we have to fill the resulting void with good. If we don't, eventually the hole will fill back in with the things we don't want there.

It's tempting sometimes to just withdraw from the world. I know there have definitely been times when I wished I could just take my family and live on some remote island where the troubles and evil of the world couldn't reach us. But we can't simply withdraw from the world, we need to stay in it and find ways to make it better! For example, instead of shunning social media because of the negativity there, we can flood it with positive, uplifting messages of truth and light! Instead of ruling out all forms of entertainment because of the rampant immorality, we can seek out the movies, books, music, etc. that are worthwhile and uplifting and support them instead.

> No ray of sunshine is ever lost, but the green that it awakens takes time to sprout, and it is not always given the sower to see the harvest.
>
> —Albert Schweitzer

TALK ABOUT IT!

1. What can I do today to bring a little more light and goodness to the world?

2. How can I be a more positive influence in my use of social media?

NOOR INAYAT KAHN: AN UNLIKELY SPY

"I do not suffer when I have to leave this world, as I have saved the freedom of my subjects. And if my death can be a lesson for you, then I am more than happy. It is not your sword which makes you a king, it is love alone."

—From *20 Jataka Tales* by Noor Inayat Kahn

NOOR INAYAT KAHN WAS BORN TO AN INDIAN FATHER, WHO WAS A Sufi preacher, and an American mother. She lived in London as a child and then moved to Paris where she spent most of her life. Noor was gentle and honest and kind, she read poetry, played music and wrote children's stories. And, due to the illness of her mother, she raised her younger siblings almost single-handedly.

When England and France declared war on Germany, Noor believed she had to do something to fight against the Nazi government and everything they stood for. She joined the Women's Auxiliary Air Force and was trained as a radio operator. From there, she was recruited by the Special Operation Executive which was a secret organization created by Winston Churchill. The S.O.E. trained spies to operate radios, provide vital information to the Allies, and participate in sabotage and resistance efforts in occupied countries.

At the S.O.E. Noor continued her radio training, including codes and radio setup. However, she was also given training on how to survive in occupied France. As a spy she wouldn't wear a uniform, and she would have no protection from the government. If she was caught, she would be shot. The average life expectancy of a radio operator was only two weeks. Noor's training was not to help her IF she got caught, but WHEN she got caught. She was taught defense techniques, disguises, weapons, how to pick a lock, how to live under an alias and how to transmit her coded messages without getting caught. Over and over again, she practiced what to say and what to do if she was caught or questioned, but many in the S.O.E. had little hope that this frail, sweet, honest girl would last long.

Finally, Noor was deemed ready. She was given the code name Madeleine and was dropped into occupied France. Noor was part of one of the largest spy networks in Paris, called the Prosper network. Disaster struck almost immediately. Within a week the top leaders were captured and the radios confiscated. Noor stayed hidden as the Germans proceeded to round up what was left of the Prosper network. Her leaders in England told her to return because it was too dangerous, but Noor, realizing she was the last radio contact with England, refused to leave.

She spent the next two months using all she had learned. She moved from place to place, setting up her radio, transmitting messages, taking it down and moving again. She had many close calls as the Gestapo became aware of her. She continually changed her appearance and moved her location to evade capture. Where the life expectancy had been two weeks, Noor survived for three months.

When Noor was caught, and was taken to prison, she immediately tried to escape. In spite of her first unsuccessful escape attempt, she tried two more times. She was repeatedly tortured and interrogated but steadfastly refused to divulge any information. On September 13, 1944, Noor was taken to Dachau concentration camp and shot as a spy. The Gestapo had not even been able to learn her real name!

Noor is remembered as one of the heroes of World War II. People were stunned by her presence of mind, her courage and her ability to outwit the Gestapo time and again. Many, seeing her before the war, would never have believed that this gentle writer of children's stories would become a war hero, but Noor's hard work and determination revealed an inner strength that could not be broken.

TRY IT!

- Choose one spiritual weapon you would like to improve in, and study it further.

- Look up scriptures about it, talk with others who are a good example of that quality,

- Think about it, pray about it and practice it.

12. AN INSTRUMENT IN GOD'S HANDS

When I was in Rome, I had the opportunity to see a lot of marble. I saw marble statues, marble columns, marble floors, marble ornaments and marble sculptures of all kinds. My favorite was a set of statues depicting Jesus Christ and the twelve apostles by Danish sculptor Bertel Thorvaldsen. They were all carved out of the most beautiful, white Carrera marble. They were stunning to look at.

Marble is one of the oldest and most beautiful stones in the world and is highly prized, but did you know that all that beautiful marble started out as limestone? Limestone is a sedimentary rock made up of several different minerals, fragments of coral and bone and other impurities. It is often used for chalk or ground into dust and added to cement. However, if intense heat and pressure is applied, the limestone can be slowly and painstakingly transformed into marble.

None of us, comparing a chunk of limestone and a beautiful marble statue, would deny that the marble is more beautiful and precious. We long to be precious and beautiful, too. Our spirits yearn for heaven and perfection. But, just as limestone can't become marble without intense heat and pressure, we can't become spiritual marble without our own periods of heat and pressure.

The refining pot is for silver, and the furnace for gold, But the Lord trieth the hearts.

—Proverbs 17:3

Think of a useful instrument like a hammer. It started out as a raw, rough piece of metal. But a raw piece of metal doesn't become useful until it is shaped into a tool or object of some kind. And guess how that is done? With intense heat & repeated hammering! The metal, just like the limestone, has to be completely changed and softened by heat and intense physical forces in order for it to become something beautiful and useful. If we want to be instruments in the Lord's hands we must allow ourselves to be shaped by Him. And this can only happen when our hearts have been softened by the intense heat of life's experiences. Jesus Christ suffered more than any other person on earth. If we want to become like Him it makes sense that we, too, will have to face the intense heat and pressure of trials and temptations.

There is no marble that was not limestone first. There is no useful tool or beautiful silver ornament that didn't start as a raw hunk of metal. If you want to become spiritual marble, you can't skip the intense heat and pressure phase. If you want to be a useful instrument in the Lord's hands, you must first endure the hammering.

The heat and pressure must be intense in order to effect the necessary change in both rock and metal, but remember, you are stronger than you think you are! You can handle more than you think you can handle! The intense heat and pressure are not going to crush you—they will turn you from limestone to marble, if you let them.

TALK ABOUT IT!

1. Our trials can make us harden our hearts and become angry if we aren't careful. What can you do to make sure that doesn't happen?

2. How does it change your attitude towards your trials, knowing that they are helping you become better prepared to make a difference?

FROM THE BIBLE: JOB, TESTED BY FIRE

Do not despise the chastening of the Almighty. For He bruises, but He binds up; He wounds, but His hands make whole.

—Job 5:17–18 (NKJV)

JOB WAS A WEALTHY AND HAPPY man. He had a wife, ten children, a large house, many servants and hundreds of animals. He was also a righteous man, who thanked God for all he had and always obeyed the commandments. Satan believed that Job was only faithful because he was so blessed. He was certain that if all Job's blessings were taken away, he would become angry at God and turn away from Him.

So God allowed Job's blessings to be taken away as a test of his faith. Servants arrived one by one with the news that his flocks had been killed or stolen, his lands had been burned and that every single one of his children had been killed. Finally, even Job's health was taken away and his skin was covered in painful boils.

Job lost everything he had. And yet, he still praised God. God was so pleased with Job and how he had gone through all of his trials with such humility and faith, that he blessed Job with twice as much as he had before!

It's no secret that lifting a feather every day won't make your muscles strong, but did you know that lifting ten pounds each day won't keep making you stronger either? That's because in order to grow stronger your muscles need to be consistently pushed beyond their current limits. If you want your muscles to keep getting stronger, you need to continually increase the weight you are lifting.

Just like our physical muscles need strengthening, our spiritual muscles need a good workout too if they are ever going to grow. Job wasn't doing anything wrong. In fact, he was doing everything right, and yet he still faced horrific trials. We will all face trials in our lives, not because the Lord doesn't love us very much but because He loves us enough to help us become more like Him.

We don't get to pick whether or not we face trials, and we don't get to decide when they come or choose which kind of trials we are given. The only thing we can choose is how we are going to react when the trials come. Are we going to harden our hearts and lose our faith, or will we let the trials soften our hearts and increase our spiritual muscle so the Lord can shape us into something beautiful?

> That the trial of your faith . . . though it be tried with
> fire, might be found unto praise and honour and glory
> at the appearing of Jesus Christ.
>
> —1 Peter 1:7

ANNIE SULLIVAN: OUT OF THE SHADOWS

"Every obstacle we overcome, every success we achieve tends to bring man closer to God and make life more as He would have it."

—Anne Sullivan

ANNE SULLIVAN WAS BORN IN 1866 IN MASSACHUSETTS. HER PARents were poor Irish immigrants trying to make a living in a new country. When Annie was five years old, she contracted an eye disease called trachoma that caused great pain in her eyes and, over time, made her nearly blind.

Then, only a few years later, her mother died from tuberculosis. After two years, Annie's father, who was an alcoholic and unable to cope with raising his children, abandoned them. Annie's youngest sister was taken in by her aunt and uncle, but no one wanted her or her little brother Jimmy. Instead, Annie and Jimmy were sent to live in a poorhouse with others who were too poor or sick to live on their own.

They suffered incredible neglect while there, playing with the rats and talking together amidst the bodies of those who died there. After only four months, Jimmy died of tuberculosis, leaving Annie completely on her own. Anne Sullivan rarely talked about her childhood, but she did say that during that dark time she wished that she could die too.

But Annie did not die. She could have chosen to waste away her life in the poorhouse, but instead she let her experiences push her to get out of there and make something of her life. When she was fourteen years old, Annie convinced a visiting inspector to take her out of the poorhouse and send her to the Perkins School for the Blind. While there, she worked hard and learned braille and the manual alphabet, which was a form of sign language that let you spell into a blind and deaf person's hand.

Meanwhile, in Alabama, the Keller family was struggling. Their young daughter, Helen, was blind and deaf and they had no idea how to help her understand or learn anything. Helen was wild and rough in her dark and silent world. She needed a special kind of teacher who not only knew how to help her, but who was just as strong-willed as she was.

Anne Sullivan became that teacher. Her determination and unique experiences helped her break through to young Helen Keller in a way that no one else could. She knew what it was like to be different, to struggle and to feel completely alone. Out of all the people who tried, it was this stubbornly courageous young woman who was able to break through Helen's silent, dark world. She taught Helen language; she taught her to spell, to read, and to speak. She became famous for what she accomplished with Helen and became Helen's companion, teacher, and friend for the rest of her life.

> Character cannot be developed in ease and quiet. Only through experience of trial and suffering can the soul be strengthened, vision cleared, ambition inspired, and success achieved.
>
> —Helen Keller

TRY IT!

- Write down some of the hard things you have gone through.

- Then think about how those difficult trials made you a better person or allowed you to be a better instrument in the Lord's hands.

A PORTRAIT IN COURAGE: THOMAS PRICE

"For love of family, for love of country, with trust in God and right, [we] made the deep commitment to protect our homes and defeat the enemy. We were, truly, a united people who appreciated what the Lord had given us and we were willing to do whatever was necessary to preserve it."

—Thomas Price

THOMAS PRICE (1924–1997): *A soldier in the United States Army 99ᵗʰ Infantry Division, Thomas fought in the Battle of the Bulge. When his commanding officers learned of the advancing German army, they decided to surrender, but nineteen-year-old Tom refused. He was sure there was more that could be done. Tom and about twelve others set out into the forest, where they set up a pocket of defense. This small group managed to hold off the advance of a German armored division and supporting infantry unit for several hours, saving the lives of many. All because one man refused to surrender.*

SECTION 4:

WHEN TIMES GET TOUGH

"Don't give up before the miracle happens."

—Annie Flagg

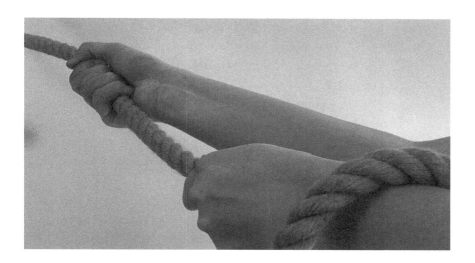

13. TRUSTING GOD

Several summers ago, my sister had a powerful experience rappelling. She writes:

When I went rappelling for the first time, I reached the top of the cliff feeling confident and excited, but when I stood up, my heart started to pound. I had not realized how high the cliff was. It hadn't looked nearly that intimidating from the ground. Doubt and fear began to grip me. Maybe I couldn't do this after all.

I looked toward the edge and was surprised to see the teenage girl who had gone ahead of me was still there. Tears were in her eyes, and I could tell right away that she was very afraid. She was already tethered to and facing our guide and instructor, who was anchored to a boulder behind him. I watched as that patient man guided her in minute detail.

"Take a step back with your left foot, now your right, good girl! Now look at me, don't look down. I've got you. I'm in control. You can throw anything at me and I can take it. I'm anchored to this big boulder, and you are anchored to me—you are secure. Hold tight to that rope. Don't ever let go. Look at me! Good girl! You can do this. I've got you. No matter what, I've got you. You won't fall. One more step back. Good girl. Wow, look at you! You are doing this! You've got perfect control. Now lean back, trust in me, trust in the rope. Your shoulders are over the edge now, good girl!"

Tears of fear were trickling down her cheeks, and as I watched her face, I prayed silently for her over and over. That leader took all the time she needed, encouraging and helping her believe in him and in herself.

She leaned a little more, moved her foot one more inch, then the next foot. And with every move she made to lean out over the edge, he cheered and encouraged her, all the time reminding her to look at him and to hold tight to the rope.

As she took that final step back and leaned out, I saw a change in her countenance. She was looking nowhere else but straight at the guide, and, in one miraculous moment, I watched the fear on her face turn to complete trust.

She slowly backed over the edge, eyes dry, looking steadily at him, as she disappeared over the edge. He kept hold and control of that rope until she made it to the bottom.

Then it was my turn. The guide tethered me to his rope and asked me to promise to not let go—no matter what. I looked at him, didn't take my eyes off his eyes, listened and obeyed, and held tight to that rope.

He gave me the same patient, loving encouragement. "Look at me. Hold tight to the rope. Keep looking at me. Good girl! You can do this. I'm right here. I'm not going anywhere. Don't let go of that rope! I've got you." I leaned backward over that cliff edge one baby step at a time and prayed. As he lowered me over the cliff and I disappeared from view, I heard his voice, calm and clear, "I'm letting you go now—But even though you can't see me, I'm still here!"

At that moment, my Heavenly Father spoke to me through this good man. I knew those words were true, that though we can't see Him, we are known and loved in a way that only our Father in Heaven can. We are His beloved children, having been taught, and prepared, and asked, and reminded, to trust

Him; and to believe that when He asks us to do something that seems more than we are capable of, there is nothing to be afraid of. If we hold tightly to the rope that tethers us to Him, we will not fail.

As I began my descent, pushing off the rocks with my feet, my vision was blurred through tears of gratitude. "My Heavenly Father loves me! He loves me!" My heart soared. I will succeed because I am not alone! And holding on to the rope, I gradually allowed myself to slide further and further away, and yet . . . ever and ever connected.

—Rachel Macdonald

TALK ABOUT IT!

1. How does knowing that God knows you and loves you, help you trust in Him?

2. Why do you think the rappelling leader asked the girls to keep their eyes on his face while they backed over the cliff?

3. The leader made the girls promise to never let go of the rope. What does the rappelling rope represent to you?

4. What can you do today to make sure you never let go of the "rope" that connects you to God?

FROM THE BIBLE: INTO THE FIRE

Our God whom we serve is able to deliver us from the burning fiery furnace.

—Daniel 3:17

THE BOOK OF DANIEL TELLS US THE STORY OF THREE FRIENDS, Shadrach, Meshach and Abednego. They were three Hebrew young men who had been taken captive into Babylon to serve King Nebuchadnezzar. The king had a giant statue made out of gold and decreed that whenever the signal sounded, everyone in the land should fall down and worship it. The punishment for disobeying this decree was death by fire.

So, all the people of the land began to worship the idol whenever the signal was given—all the people except the three friends. When the king was told of their disobedience, he was furious. He commanded that Shadrach, Meshach, and Abednego be brought before him. He asked them about the rumors, and they boldly stated that they were true.

The king offered them another chance, saying that if they would fall down and worship the idol from now on, all would be forgiven and they would not have to die. But, he said, if you do not, I will throw you into the fiery furnace. To this threat, the three friends boldly replied, "Our God whom we serve is able to deliver us from the burning fiery furnace . . . but if not, be it known unto thee, O king, that we will not serve thy gods, nor worship the golden image which thou hast set up" (Daniel 3:17–18).

At that, the king ordered the friends bound with strong ropes. He was so angry that he ordered the furnace to be made seven times hotter than usual. It was so hot, that the men who threw them into the flames died from the heat that came just from standing close to it. Shadrach, Meshach and Abednego were thrown into the flames, firmly bound. Their death seemed assured; it did not appear that God was going to save them. But they remained calm and faithful.

Then, a moment after they had been thrown into the flames the king cried out in wonder. Instead of three bound men burning, he saw four men, unbound, walking unharmed amongst the flames. And he said the fourth man looked like the Son of God. The King called out to them, to come out of the flames. And when they came out, they were completely unharmed. Not even their clothing smelled like smoke.

> And the Lord shall help them, and deliver them: He shall deliver them from the wicked, and save them, because they trust in Him.
>
> —Psalm 37:40

Shadrach, Meshach, and Abednego didn't know ahead of time that they would be protected from the flames. Sometimes, because we are so familiar with the story, we forget that. They trusted that the Lord was on their side and that He would protect them, if it was right.

It took a lot of faith and trust for Shadrach, Meshach and Abednego to boldly tell the king that God could miraculously save them from burning in a fiery furnace. But it's

> Who shall separate us from the love of Christ? Shall tribulation, or distress, or persecution, or famine, or nakedness, or peril, or sword? . . . Nay, in all these things we are more than conquerors through Him that loved us.
>
> —Romans 8:35, 37

what they said next that demonstrates the true strength of their trust in God. After boldly stating their belief in miracles they told the king that even if God did not protect them, they would still refuse to bow to the idols. Even if the Lord did not save them, they still loved Him, they still worshiped Him, and they still trusted that He loved them and that whatever happened would be for the best.

It takes a great deal of faith to believe in miracles, but it can take even more faith to trust that God is still there, when the miracles don't seem to come. When we see the answers to our prayers immediately and obviously, it is easy to believe God is listening. How much more difficult is it to believe when our prayers seem to go unanswered; when our lives seem to be falling apart, no matter how hard we try to do what is right, and when blessings and answers seem a long time in coming?

In those times, we can remember the faith of Shadrach, Meshach, and Abednego, who did not see the miracle until after they were thrown into the furnace, until after they continued to believe, even when there seemed to be no reason why they should. Like them, we can say, "I believe in God. I believe that He loves me. I believe that He has heard my prayers and is answering them, even if I cannot see it."

TALK ABOUT IT!

1. Psalm 37:40 says God will "save them because they trust in Him." If that doesn't mean we will always be physically protected if we have faith in God, what does it mean? How will He save us?

2. Why do you think Shadrach, Meshach, and Abednego didn't just bow down and pretend to worship the idol in order to stay safe?

3. Often when we are trying to do what is right, things get harder, rather than easier. Why do you think that is? What can you do to prepare to face that?

CORRIE TEN BOOM: ANSWERED PRAYERS

"Never be afraid to trust an unknown future to a known God."

—Corrie Ten Boom

CORRIE TEN BOOM WAS BORN INTO A DEVOUT CHRISTIAN FAMILY who taught her the importance of loving and helping others. So, when the Nazis invaded the Netherlands in May 1940, the Ten Boom family decided they had to do something to help protect the Dutch Jews.

They created a tiny, hidden room, no bigger than a closet in Corrie's bedroom. The space was large enough to hold six people, but only if they stood up straight the entire time. A false wall was built in front to hide it.

Whenever a Nazi patrol came around, one of the Ten Booms would press a hidden buzzer to alert the Jews staying with them. The Jews would then have less than a minute to quickly and quietly get into the hiding place and close it up. Some of the Jews would only stay with the Ten

> Trust in the Lord, with all thine heart. And lean not unto thine own understanding. In all thy ways, acknowledge Him, and He shall direct thy paths.
>
> —Proverbs 3:5–6

Booms for a few hours and some for a few days, before being moved on to more permanent places.

During the next few years, Corrie and her family used their watch shop and home above to become heavily involved in the Dutch resistance, and to help save the lives of around 800 Jews. They were doing something to fight against the evil of their day and it felt good. Corrie could see the good they were doing and constantly prayed that they would be protected so they could continue their work.

However, on February 28, 1944 the Ten Booms were betrayed by a Dutch informant and were all arrested by the Nazis. Her eighty-five-year-old father died in prison and Corrie prayed that she and her sister, Betsie, would not be sent to a German concentration camp, but that prayer also seemed to go unanswered. She and Betsie were sent to the notorious Ravensbrück concentration camp. It did not seem like the Lord had answered her prayers at all. Corrie was angry at God. She struggled and felt abandoned.

But then, something interesting began to happen. She and Betsie were able to get ahold of a smuggled Bible. They began reading from it daily to the other ladies in the camp who would listen. They taught, prayed, and helped strengthened everyone around them.

When Betsie died after six months in the camp, Corrie continued the work alone. At the end of the war, when Corrie was finally freed, she wrote a book about her experiences called *The Hiding Place*. She began to speak to groups all over the world, sharing the messages of faith, forgiveness, and Jesus Christ with thousands upon thousands of people.

The Lord had not been ignoring her prayers for protection. He was answering them. But He was answering them in a much bigger and more lasting way than Corrie had been thinking.

Her desires had been to help save people from physical death, which she did for a time, but God blessed her with the opportunity to help save many, many others from spiritual death. And by leading her through those difficult experiences, He was making the way possible for her to reach people all over the world, not just in her hometown and country.

If she had helped save Jews in her hometown and was never caught, we might have heard of her. But it is the fact that she was caught and sent to a concentration camp, it's the fact that she held to her faith under such difficult circumstances that makes her story so powerful!

The protection the Lord promises is not always physical, not always obvious, and not always the way we want it to be, but it is always given. Trust that the Lord knows the desires of your heart and that if you trust in Him, he will help you make a difference in a way even greater and more lasting than you can now imagine.

COMMIT TODAY TO TRUST IN THE LORD—NO MATTER WHAT.

TRY IT!

- Can you think of a time in your life when it seemed like God wasn't answering your prayers?

- Looking back, can you see how He was helping you, even though you couldn't see it? Write about it in your journal so you don't forget.

- Find a quote, a picture, or Bible verse that reminds you to trust in God. Put it where you can see it often.

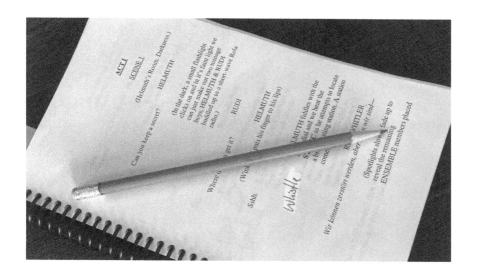

14. JUST DO YOUR BEST

When I was putting on the first fully staged production of my play, *Resistance Movement*, I didn't have the money to pay for professional actors or a theatre where we could put it on. The play tells the true story of the Hübener group, three German teenagers who had the courage to stand against Hitler. I knew the story had the power to inspire and change people, so I prayed to know the best way to present it. As I prayed, I felt like it was important to continue with the production even without professional resources.

We got permission to use our local church, my husband built the sets, and I gathered some actor friends and other church members to play most of the roles. However, I still needed someone for the lead role of fifteen-year-old Rudi. The role of Rudi was demanding emotionally, plus he was in every single scene! I agonized over who to cast in this crucial role but could think of no one. Then one day, while pondering over what I should do, the name of a young man I knew at church came into my mind, and I felt the clear impression that I should cast him as Rudi.

He was stunned when I asked him to play the role. Ben was sixteen and had only played small parts in a school play or two. He also told me he was terrible at memorizing lines. I was a bit nervous, but I knew what I had felt. He was extremely nervous, but I convinced him to give it a shot anyway.

The only available time for us to do the performance at the church was a mere two weeks away. We jumped into rehearsing, and Ben gave it everything he had. He worked on memorizing his part constantly, but the week of the performance arrived, and Ben still couldn't remember his lines.

> **Excellence is not being the best; it is doing your best.**

I decided that we would perform the most important and emotional scenes fully memorized but that we would hold our scripts for the other scenes. My hope was that Ben would be able to memorize his lines better with fewer scenes to worry about. I admit I was a bit disappointed because it wasn't the way I had dreamed of seeing the play, but I felt it was worth it to relieve the pressure on Ben so he could focus on his performance instead of on remembering his lines.

The day of the performance came, and we were getting ready for our first and only dress rehearsal that afternoon. To be completely honest, we were not ready. The lines were just not there. Ben, and even several of the other actors, were still having trouble with the scenes that were supposed to be memorized.

We got ready and prayed fervently together that the Spirit would be with us and that we would be able to remember the things we needed to. Then we began our final rehearsal. The first scene went flawlessly; then the second and third scenes as well. By the time we reached the end of the play, we realized that we had done the entire thing without any scripts at all! Even the scenes we had planned on using our scripts for had been memorized!

> **When you live to make a difference, God will make up the difference between your abilities and your desires.**

Two hours later we went on for our first performance and did the entire show without any scripts at all. And not only that, we didn't forget a single line! It truly was a miracle. Ben and the rest of us had given it everything we had, and then the Lord took our offering and made it far beyond what we could do by ourselves.

FROM THE BIBLE: THE WIDOW'S MITE

I say unto you that this poor widow hath cast in more than they all: for all these have of their abundance cast in unto the offerings of God: but she . . . cast in all the living she had.

—Luke 21:3–4

ONE DAY, WHILE JESUS WAS teaching in the temple, he saw the people coming and giving their offerings to the temple treasury. He watched as each individual came and cast various amounts of money into the treasury. Many of the people there were rich, and some gave quite a bit of money. Then, out of the crowd, came a poor widow with her offering. As she held out her hand Jesus and the crowd could see that she had in her palm only two small mites. A mite was the smallest coin available and two of them together equaled only about a penny.

When Jesus saw this he said to the people that this poor widow had given more than all the rest. He explained that although the others had given larger amounts of money, this woman had given everything she had. It was not the largest amount, but it was the largest sacrifice.

She might have been embarrassed to put so little into the treasury. I'm sure she wished she had more to give. Perhaps she wondered if her measly two mites would even make a difference. Maybe she wondered if they were even worth giving at all. But Jesus, when he saw her offering, praised it and let the multitude know that it was enough.

His response teaches us that it is more about the sacrifice than the amount we give. Others gave so much more money, but they had more to give. The widow only had two mites and yet she gave it all. Others around us may have more money to donate, more time, health or resources to give. They may be more talented and have greater opportunities to make a difference than we do. We may only be able to give our two mites to the cause. But this story reminds us that if we sacrifice what we have to serve Him—no matter how little, it will be enough.

Did you know that a honeybee spends its whole life working, only to make a quarter teaspoon of honey? Their entire life's work produces only that tiny bit of honey! But I don't think anyone of us would say that that honey bee's life is useless or that they make so little honey, they might as well not make any honey at all. And yet, we convince ourselves that our small contributions to the world are too insignificant to matter.

The glory of the honeybee is not in the amount of honey it produces but in the way all the bees work together to produce something wonderful! The same can be said of us. Our worth doesn't come from how much of a difference we make. It doesn't matter if our efforts convert hundreds or only one. Maybe we work our whole lives, trying to do what's right, trying to be a good example and trying to make the world a better place, only to realize that we have only made a tiny ¼ teaspoon of difference. It simply does not matter. What does matter is that we TRY. That's all that God asks of us. He does not ask us to be successful in making a difference, instead he asks us to keep ourselves worthy and put ourselves in the position where He will be able to make a difference through us.

Don't judge your efforts by how much effect you have, but on how fully your heart is turned to God.

TALK ABOUT IT!

1. Do you ever feel like your efforts or talents aren't enough? What have you learned from these three examples that might help you overcome that?

2. Why do we think the big things are more important than the small ones?

3. How does being grateful for your efforts and abilities help you see them the way God sees them?

WALLACE HARTLEY:
BANDMASTER OF THE TITANIC

"I've always felt that when men are called to face death suddenly, music is more effective in cheering them on than all the firearms in creation."

—Wallace Hartley

WALLACE HARTLEY WAS THIRTY-THREE YEARS OLD AND RECENTLY engaged to be married when he became the first violinist and band-master on the Titanic. The ship's maiden voyage was just a few months before his wedding, and his fiancée had even given him the violin he played on that fateful voyage.

On the night of April 14th, the band had finished for the night when the Titanic struck an iceberg, ripping a hole down the side of the ship. As the ship began to fill with water, it became apparent that the Titanic was going to sink. People began flocking to the lifeboats, but there were 2,200 people on board and room in the lifeboats for only half that number!

Wallace Hartley saw the fear and panic in the people around him and wanted to help. He couldn't stop the Titanic from sinking. He couldn't provide more lifeboats or somehow save all the people on board; he was just a musician. However, he could do his best to bring them comfort. So, Wallace and the other band members gathered together on the deck and began to play. They played and played as the Titanic sank beneath them and the people struggled around them.

Finally, Wallace put his violin in its case and sank with the ship. Not a single member of the band survived.

Their offering may have seemed small compared to what they wished they could do. I'm sure they wished they could save people's lives somehow, but they couldn't. They could, however, try to comfort their spirits. Instead of feeling sorry for themselves because they couldn't do something bigger, they simply did what they could. Their music brought comfort and peace to many that night, and their story has brought inspiration to many more in the years since. And all they did was play a little music.

JUST DO THE BEST YOU CAN. NO ONE CAN DO MORE THAN THAT.

TRY IT!

Next time you feel that you aren't enough and that you don't measure up:

- Do your best to focus on your efforts and not on the outcome.

- Do everything you can and then watch with faith for the Lord to make up the difference.

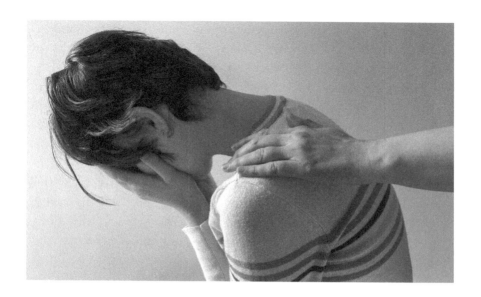

15. YOU'RE NEVER ALONE!

Several years ago, I was having a difficult time in my life. I had just finished a hard pregnancy and then after the birth, I imme-diately began struggling with postpartum depression. And on top of it all, our new baby would not sleep. Ever. She would fall asleep and then minutes later, she would wake up crying. I would finally get her back to sleep and then just as I was falling asleep, she would wake up again, and the whole process would repeat itself—all night long. She wouldn't even nap during the day, so neither one of us got any sleep. Eventually I just dragged a sleeping bag into my baby's room at night because it wasn't worth it to go back to my own bed.

I was so exhausted, physically and emotionally. I would talk with a friend or family member on the phone and pretend like everything was fine because I didn't want them to get tired of my crying or complaining. But then I would hang up the phone and sob on the floor. I prayed and prayed, pleading for answers and help, but nothing changed. If anything, it got worse.

Then one particularly difficult night, I just felt like I couldn't handle it anymore. I remember being awake with the baby in the middle of the night and it felt like I was the only one in the whole world who was awake. I felt so utterly and completely alone. I began to pray, but I felt nothing. I was tired of pleading and praying without feeling peace or answers of any kind. For the first time in my life, I truly wondered if God was even real. I felt I was alone, not just in the world, but alone in the universe. I felt despair.

I finally got my baby back to sleep and laid her in the crib. I fell to my knees again and begged God one more time. But this time, I didn't ask Him to take away my problems, or to help the baby sleep. I simply asked if He was real, if He was there and if He knew me. Before I could finish my prayer, the baby woke up and began crying. Again. I stood up and, weary to my very soul, I leaned over the crib and put my hand on my crying baby. I could not summon up enough energy to do anything else.

As I stood there, with my hand on my baby, I suddenly felt someone standing behind me in the exact same position as I was, with their hand on the baby's chest. The baby instantly stopped crying and fell back asleep. The feeling was so strong and distinct. I felt that if I turned around, I would see someone there. But I didn't feel like I should look, so I just stood there, holding my breath until the feeling slowly faded. The room was still and quiet and everyone else in the world might still have been asleep, but I knew I was not alone. I was filled with peace and love.

I wish I could tell you that from that point on, my baby had no trouble sleeping, but that's not the case. It still took a couple months after that to figure out what was going on and to get the treatment we needed so the baby could sleep. It still wasn't easy, but I knew that God was real. I knew that He knew me. And I knew that He loved me.

FROM THE BIBLE: AN ARMY OF ANGELS

For He shall give His angels charge over you, To keep you in all your ways. In their hands they shall bear you up.

—Psalm 91:11–12
(NKJV)

IN 2 KINGS THERE IS THE STORY of a Syrian king who wanted to defeat the Israelite army. He kept sending the Syrian army to attack, but each time the Israelite army was warned ahead of time by the prophet Elisha, and the attacks were unsuccessful. Angry and determined to defeat the Israelites, the King of Syria ordered his army to kidnap Elisha so he couldn't keep ruining their plans.

During the night, the Syrian army surrounded the city where Elisha was staying. In the morning, Elisha's servant woke up and began preparing for the day. When he stepped outside the tent, he was horrified to see that they were completely surrounded by a massive army!

In a panic, he woke up Elisha and asked him what they should do. When Elisha saw what had happened, he said to his servant, "Fear not: for they that be with us are more than they that be with them" (2 Kings 6:16).

The servant looked at the hills and could only see the Syrian army, but Elisha prayed and asked God to open the young man's eyes. And this time, when the servant looked, he could see a huge army of angels, horses and chariots of fire, completely surrounding them, protecting them from the enemy.

Just like Elisha, you have angels surrounding you, ready to protect and help you! There is an unseen army of people both on the earth and in the heavens who are fighting on your side. They are fighting with you and for you. When you are trying to do what's right, you are never alone!

> Fear thou not; for I am with thee: be not dismayed; for I am thy God: I will strengthen thee; yea, I will help thee; yea, I will uphold thee with the right hand of my righteousness.
>
> —Isaiah 41:10

TALK ABOUT IT!

1. How does it make you feel knowing that you are surrounded by angels? Does it change the way you act?

2. Why do you think God doesn't let us see the angels around us all the time?

V FOR VICTORY!

"The V for victory is the symbol of the unconquerable will of the occupied territories. As long as we have faith in our own cause, and the unconquerable will to win, victory will not be denied us."

—Winston Churchill

DURING WORLD WAR II THE NAZI GOVERNMENT TRIED TO MAKE anyone who was anti-Nazi think they were the only ones who felt that way. They did this because they knew how powerful their opponents could become if they were united and hopeful.

Because it was so dangerous to talk openly against the Nazi government, the Allies came up with a way to secretly recognize others who were against Hitler. It was started by the Belgians, and quickly taken up by Winston Churchill, and it was known as the V for Victory!

The campaign was spread through radio broadcasts to Allies throughout all Nazi-occupied countries. The people began wearing the V as jewelry or buttons, painting it on walls, fences and posters, stamping it on envelopes and writing it anywhere they could. The Morse code for the letter V is three short taps and one long. It sounds like the first few notes of Beethoven's

fifth symphony, so people began whistling the tune wherever they went. They even began knocking on their friend's doors in Morse code. In this way the V became the symbol of all who opposed Hitler and brought comfort and hope to many.

The enemy today—Satan—also wants you to feel like you are the only one who feels the way you do. He wants you to feel discouraged and like you are the only one who is trying to do any good. He loves it when you feel hopeless and afraid. Your fear and despair are some of his greatest weapons because he knows that if you feel hopeless and afraid, you will stop trying so hard to stop him.

So reach out and support and strengthen one another in your efforts! Do not despair at the darkness and evil in the world; do not accept as truth the lie that you are the only one who feels like you do. I promise you that there are many, many others. Find them so you can support one another in your efforts. And know that even if you never meet another soul who feels the way you do. God sees you. He knows you and is helping you. You are not alone.

TRY IT!

- See how many scripture verses you can find that remind you God and His angels are with you.

- Highlight or mark them so every time you open your Bible you are reminded that you are never alone!

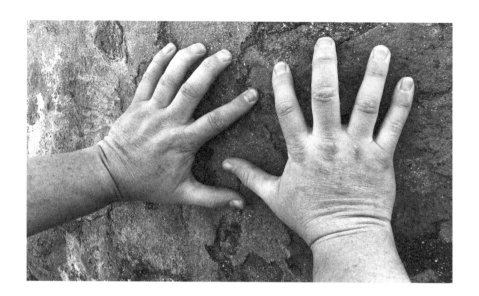

16. WHEN YOU FEEL LIKE A FAILURE

Once upon a time, there was a man who was sleeping at night in his cabin when suddenly his room filled with light and the Savior appeared. The Lord told the man He had work for him to do and showed him a large rock in front of his cabin. The Lord explained that the man was to push against the rock with all his might. This the man did, day after day. For many years he toiled from sun up to sun down, his shoulders set squarely against the cold, massive surface of the unmoving rock, pushing with all his might.

Each night the man returned to his cabin sore and worn out, feeling that his whole day had been spent in vain. Seeing that the man was showing signs of discouragement, Satan decided to enter the picture placing thoughts into the man's mind such as: "You have been pushing against that rock for a long time, and it hasn't budged. Why kill yourself over this? You are never going to move it."

"Lord," the man said, "I have labored long and hard in your service, giving all my strength to do what you have asked. Yet, after all this time, I have not even budged that rock a half a millimeter. What is wrong? Why am I failing?" To this the Lord responded compassionately, "My child, when long ago I asked you to serve me, and you accepted, I told you that your task was to push against the rock with all your strength, which you have done. Never once did I mention to you that I expected you to move it. Your task was to push.

"And now you come to me, your strength spent, thinking that you have failed. But, is that really so? Look at yourself. Your arms are strong and muscled, your hands are calloused from constant pressure, and your legs have become massive and strong. Through opposition, you have grown much and your abilities now surpass that which you used to have. You haven't moved the rock, but your calling was to be obedient and to push and to exercise your faith and trust in my wisdom. This you have done. I, my child, will now move the rock."

TRY IT!

- Next time you feel like you are not moving the rocks in your life, see if you can find any blessings that have come to you because you are trying.

- Write them down and focus on the positive outcomes instead of the things you feel didn't work out.

FROM THE BIBLE: THE WEEPING PROPHET

O my soul, my soul! I am pained in my very heart!

—Jeremiah 4:19, 22 (NKJV)

IN THE OLD TESTAMENT, God called Jeremiah to be a prophet. Jeremiah was stunned. He was only about seventeen years old and had no experience as a prophet or in speaking to the people. He immediately told God that he couldn't do it. But God told Jeremiah not to be afraid because He would be with him. God said He would put His words in Jeremiah's mouth so he would know what to say. God then told Jeremiah what he wanted him to do. Jeremiah was charged with commanding the Israelites to repent or they would soon be destroyed.

Jeremiah began his work. For four decades he preached and taught and warned the people. But the people rejected him and his message. They ignored him, laughed at him, arrested him, put him in dungeons, and finally stoned him. For forty years they refused to listen to his message. Jeremiah became known as "The Weeping Prophet" because of all the tears he shed over the people of Israel who would not listen to God's message. He was the last prophet and final warning before the nation of Judah was destroyed by God. He gave his life to the cause, but nothing changed. No one listened or repented and the people were destroyed.

I'm sure Jeremiah felt like a failure more than once. Maybe he wondered if the people would have listened to him better if he had done things differently or was a better speaker. Maybe he felt like he had let God down. And if Jeremiah's calling was to make the people repent then I guess he would be a failure. But if we look closely at the story, God never asked him to make the Israelites repent. He simply asked him to teach and warn them, and that is exactly what Jeremiah did. He cried and struggled, but he didn't give up, even though his efforts must have seemed ridiculously ineffective at times. That is not failure, it is success!

Think of a lighthouse. It can't force sailors to follow it's light and stay safe, it can only shine it's light into the darkness the best it can. And if someone does not pay attention to the lighthouse and crashes on the rocks, we certainly don't blame the lighthouse.

Remember that you, too, are like the lighthouse. You cannot force people to accept the light that you share, and that isn't even what God has asked of you. All you can do is shine your light into the darkness in the best way you know how. Then trust in God, to bring them safely to the shore.

> Refrain thy voice from weeping, and thine eyes from tears: for thy work shall be rewarded, saith the Lord.
>
> —Jeremiah 31:16

THE HÜBENER GROUP: TEENS AGAINST HITLER

"Now I must die, even though I have committed no crime . . . I know that God lives and He will be the Just Judge in this matter . . . I look forward to seeing you in a better world!"

—Helmuth Hübener

HELMUTH HÜBENER, KARL-HEINZ SCHNIBBE AND RUDI WOBBE were three friends who went to the same church. In 1941 Karl was seventeen years old, Helmuth was sixteen, and Rudi was fifteen. When the Nazis took over Germany and the rest of Europe, these three did not like what they saw. The news at the time was completely controlled by the Nazi party. All radio stations and news sources from outside of Germany were banned. And the consequences for disobeying those laws were steep: imprisonment or death.

But Helmuth knew that the news he was hearing from the government did not add up. He got ahold of a shortwave radio, which could pick up radio stations from outside of Germany and began listening to BBC London. Soon he invited Rudi and Karl to listen with him. As World War II worsened, and they saw friends and neighbors disappear, simply because they were Jewish or because they spoke out against the Nazis or their methods, the three boys determined that knowing the truth wasn't enough. They had to spread it.

They began meeting in Helmuth's attic late at night, listening to the BBC London, typing up what they heard into anti-Nazi leaflets, and distributing them around Hamburg. They stuffed them in mailboxes, under doorways, into coat pockets, and even posted them on the official Nazi bulletin boards! They were excited and felt like they were really doing something. Rudi was sure they were going to be heroes!

But after about six months, they were suddenly caught by the Gestapo. All three were brutally interrogated, beaten and half starved for months in prison before being sent before the Nazi court known as the "Blood Tribunal" for sentencing. Karl was sentenced to five years in a labor camp. Rudi was sentenced to ten years in a labor camp. And Helmuth, as the leader, was sentenced to death.

They had only a few moments together in a holding cell before they were parted forever. Can you imagine what they must have felt? They had sacrificed so much, and for what? They had lost everything and had been turned in by some of the very people they were trying to help. They hadn't brought down the Nazi government. As far as they knew, they hadn't even made a dent in it, or changed a single person's mind. They sat there, alone and afraid, feeling like they had completely failed.

Their little resistance movement most likely did not have much of an effect on Germany or the war at all. But as they sat there in despair, thinking they had failed, they could not see the thousands of lives their story would touch. They could not see the generations of their families who would be strengthened by their faith and courage. They could not see the young mom, whose life would be saved by the hearing and sharing of their story, or the young man in juvenile detention whose hope was rekindled by their faith. They could not see the countless people around the world who would hear of their courage and determine to do a little more to stand for truth.

My friends, they may not have succeeded in the way they had originally planned, but they most certainly did NOT fail.

The only way to fail is to stop trying.

TALK ABOUT IT!

1. Why do you think God told Jeremiah to warn the people to repent, even though He knew the people wouldn't listen?

2. None of the people in these examples failed in God's eyes, but their idea of success was different from God's. How can you redefine success for yourself?

WILL YOU JOIN US?

DURING THE AMERICAN CIVIL WAR, THE ARMIES USED A UNIQUE kind of soldier. These soldiers would lead the charge, carrying the army's flag. They were vital for showing the army which way to go, when to charge and when to retreat or change tactics. They also helped boost the company's morale by reminding them of the land and people they were fighting for. Because of their importance, the flag bearer became a favorite target of the enemy. They knew that if they could shoot down the flag bearer, the rest of the army might become disorganized, disheartened and ineffective.

It became a great honor to be the flag bearer. Each flag bearer was surrounded by the flag guard, who were committed to keeping the flag bearer safe. When the flag bearer was shot, another would instantly run forward, pick up the flag, and continue the charge.

There have been many courageous flag bearers throughout history, who have led the charge in the fight for a better world. They have stood for truth and valiantly fought against the evil of their day. But they are now gone. We need new flag bearers to set the world ablaze with light and truth.

The battle flag is lying at your feet . . .

WILL YOU PICK IT UP?

WILL YOU HOLD ON TO IT WITH ALL YOU HAVE AND RUN INTO BATTLE?

It will not be easy, but it will be worth it. Remember that when we are striving to do what's right and make the world a better place, there is no such thing as failure. Remember that light cannot fail to dissipate the darkness.

Remember that God, our loving Father in Heaven, sees your efforts. He knows you. He loves you, and He is guiding you. And when you see Him again, He will enfold you in His arms and say to you, "Well done, thou good and faithful servant."

I cannot prove to you that the things you have read here are true. That is something you can do only for yourself. I can only tell you with every fiber of my being that I believe them to be so. And I challenge you to prove the principles here. Put them into practice and see what comes from it. If the results are good, then these words are of God. If the results are evil then they are not. There is no third option.

If you find that these things are true and of God, do everything you can to stand forth and proclaim these truths with power and faith, and I promise you that God, your loving Father in Heaven, who knows you and loves you, will be with you and that He will multiply your efforts beyond what you can foresee.

Begin today. Get down on your knees and ask God if these things are true. Ask Him if He knows you and loves you. Ask Him if He has a work for you to do. And then ask Him to help you discover what that is. And if you do not receive an answer immediately—DO NOT GIVE UP. I promise you that He will answer in his own time and in his own way.

'Til we meet in the Resistance!

A PORTRAIT IN COURAGE:
IRENA SENDLER

"To save one Jewish child, ten Poles and two Jews had to risk death. To betray that same child and the family that hid him required only one informer or, worse still, one blackmailer. The risk of being caught by the SS was not prison, but death—death for the entire family. But I was taught that if you see a person drowning, you must jump in to save them, whether you can swim or not."

—Irena Sendler

IRENA SENDLER (1910–2008): *Polish social worker and nurse who volunteered with the Polish Resistance in German-occupied Warsaw. Irena helped organize the rescue of an estimated 2,500 Jewish children from the Warsaw Ghetto. She smuggled them out in a variety of ways, provided them with fake identity papers and found them safe places to live. In 1943 Irena was arrested, sent to prison, and tortured, but she managed to continue to hide the names and locations of the smuggled children. On the day of her scheduled execution, she was rescued and set free by fellow resistance fighters, who had bribed the guards who were escorting her. She changed her identity and immediately resumed her work with the Jewish children in the ghetto.*

APPENDIX
★ ★ ★

TROUBLESHOOTING INDEX

1. I'M SO BUSY. HOW CAN I FIND THE TIME TO MAKE A DIFFERENCE?

One of the biggest lies we tell ourselves is that we don't have enough time or money to do the things we really want. How many of us have said things like, "I wish I had time to read more"; "I wish I could travel"; "I wish I had time to be more involved in my community"; or "I wish I could afford to be more generous"? But they remain wishes because we tell ourselves we don't have the time, the money, or other resources.

I recently saw a quote that said, "The first step toward getting what you want is having the courage to get rid of what you don't." This is definitely true. We can't do it all at the same time, so choices must be made. However, most of us don't have too hard a time getting rid of things we don't want at all. The greater difficulty seems to lie in sacrificing things we want for things we want more. So perhaps it might be better to say, "The first step toward getting what you want is having the courage to get rid of the things you want less."

My husband and I decided we want to travel more. So we sold our house and moved into a townhome. I took on some extra work, and we sold one of our cars. A while later we found a great deal on tickets and booked a trip to Rome. It was a wonderful trip. When we returned home, we had several people say things like, "Wow, I wish I could take a trip like that. I would love to travel, but I can't afford it." The interesting thing is that my husband and I weren't making any more money than the people who said that. In several cases we were even making less. We simply chose to spend our money in different ways. I explained how we had sold our home, and taken on extra work to be able to go, and encouraged them, saying that if they really wanted to travel, they could find a way to make it possible too. However, most of them turned away uninterested. They wanted to travel but didn't want it enough to give up anything they already had to get it.

Most of us want to have a positive impact on the world, but how many of us are willing to sacrifice something else in order to do it? When we say we don't have the time or resources, what we're really saying is that these things are not enough of a priority right now for us to make the time to do them.

I'm not saying that we should be running ourselves ragged or going into debt to do it all. There is nothing wrong with having priorities—in fact we need to prioritize because we simply cannot do everything. What I am saying, is that we need to make sure we are intentionally choosing our priorities rather than having them chosen for us by default. We need to make sure that we're not missing out on what is truly important to us because we're filling our time and using our resources in pursuit of things that are less important.

It's not possible to find the time to do everything. But it is possible to make the time to do what is truly important to us—IF we are willing to sacrifice some of the things we want less.

Today, take a minute and think about what is really important to you. Then ask yourself, "Do my current priorities support that?" If not, have the courage to let go of the things you want less, so you can fill your life with the things you want more.

THINGS WHICH MATTER MOST, MUST NEVER BE AT THE MERCY OF THINGS WHICH MATTER LEAST.

—JOHANN WOLFGANG VON GOETHE

2. HOW CAN I TELL IF WHAT I THINK/FEEL IS THE HOLY SPIRIT OR MY OWN MIND?

I remember when I was a teenager, and I had a thought to do something nice for someone in my neighborhood. I was a little nervous about it because I didn't know him well and I wanted to make sure it was the right thing before I risked embarrassing myself. I asked my mom how I could know if this thought I had was just my own mind or if it was inspired from God. She told me that if it was something that was kind, loving, thoughtful, or good in any way, it was from God because all good things come from Him.

So I acted on the thought I had, and it turned out to be a really wonderful experience. From then on, I never had to wonder if a thought I had was "inspired" or not. I simply held it up to that same test. If it was good, I knew it was from God, and I acted on it.

In the New Testament, James echoes what my mother said: "Every good gift and every perfect gift is from above, and cometh down from the father of lights, with whom is no variableness, neither shadow of turning" (James 1:17). All good gifts come from God! Think of it! Every beautiful sight, every sound, every taste, every experience, every thought, every feeling that is good, comes from our Father in Heaven.

Inspiration can come in many forms. It can come as a thought that pops into your head, something that you read or hear that hits you with particular power, guidance from scripture and parents and leaders. It could be that social media post you've felt like you should make, that book idea you've had for years, that melody you find yourself humming, a service project you've had an idea for, or that person you keep thinking you should call.

Sometimes inspiration comes quickly and easily. Sometimes it feels like you have to wrestle it into place. But in all cases, the same test applies: Is it leading me to do good? Will this action benefit others? If the answer is yes, it is from God.

Each day, pray to know who you can help or what you can do to make a difference that day. Then go forward, looking for opportunities to do good, paying close attention to the thoughts and promptings you receive.

3. I CAN'T SEEM TO FIND THE RIGHT BALANCE BETWEEN ALL I NEED TO DO.

Usually when we think about balance, we picture a set of scales or a teeter-totter, right? We think that both sides have to have the same amount of weight on them in order for the scale to be in balance. Another image that comes to mind when we think of balance, is standing on one leg and trying to keep from falling over or putting your other foot down.

However, using these analogies we can actually wear ourselves out by running back and forth trying to add or take away weight to each side, in order to achieve perfect balance. Or we can stress ourselves out by trying to hold everything at once without putting our other "foot" down.

Instead, think of balance as a bicycle wheel. Each spoke represents something you want in your life: social activities, time to study the scriptures, sleep, a hobby you want to develop, chores that need to be done, etc. All of these things are important so they are all on the wheel, but not all the spokes point straight up at once, right? The wheel turns and, as it does, different things take their turn at the top of the wheel and become the priority, while other things take their turn at the bottom.

When I am writing or working on a huge project, people always ask me how I manage to fit it all in, but the answer is that I don't! When a project or goal is the top priority, other things have to give a little. When I was training for my black belt, my girls ate a lot of chicken nuggets for dinner and my laundry pile looked like Mt. Everest!

Balance isn't doing everything at once in perfect balance, it is allowing the things you want to do to take their turn as the top priority, while allowing other things to take their turn at the bottom.

4. I FEEL SO ALONE. WHY DON'T I FEEL GOD WITH ME IN MY STRUGGLES?

When I was making the film about the Hübener Group (pg. 147), I had cast a young man named Joey to play the lead role of Rudi. At the end of the film, after being arrested, Rudi faces his future alone in prison. At this point in the film, Rudi has to reach that extreme depth of loneliness and pain that is despair and heartbreak. The scene in the film is only a few minutes, but it took us two and a half hours to film it.

So, in order to film the scene, Joey had to open himself up to feeling that deep loneliness and pain for the entire two and a half hours. Joey was extremely nervous to film this scene. It takes a lot of courage to allow others to see your deepest emotional pain, and to do it for so long was absolutely terrifying. I had come to care for Joey very much throughout the process of rehearsing and filming and it broke my heart to have to make him suffer for so long. I could hardly stand to see him broken and sobbing for so long. Every part of me wanted to just yell "Cut!" and rush over and stop his pain, but I knew that if this last scene wasn't right, the film wouldn't work, and all Joey's previous efforts and sacrifices would have been for nothing. So, I continued, unable to comfort him.

Usually, I watch what is being filmed through the monitor, but this time, I was kneeling on the floor beside him, as close as I could possibly get without being in the shot. He could not see that I was right there crying with him. I couldn't touch him or stop the pain or comfort him in any way because if I did, he wouldn't be able to complete the emotional journey necessary to make the scene meaningful. He couldn't see me, but I was crying and suffering with him through every moment. I never left his side.

The instant we finally got all the shots we needed, I rushed in and hugged him tightly while the crew changed the lighting and cameras around us. He had done it! I held him as we cried and laughed and prayed together. It was a moment I will never forget.

Dear friends, sometimes it is necessary for us to feel like we are alone in order for us to learn and grow. Sometimes He allows our trials to go on far longer than we think we can stand, and we are sure that He has forgotten us. But remember, even though He sometimes allows us to feel alone, we NEVER actually are! God is there, right beside you, crying with you, loving you and supporting you always!

5. WHAT DO I DO WHEN I START TO DOUBT GOD IS REAL?

The Apostle Paul was on board a ship during a storm. To prevent capsizing, they lowered their sails and let themselves be driven by the wind. However, that wasn't enough, so they had to lighten the ship by throwing heavy things overboard. The account goes on to say that the storm was so bad they couldn't see the sun or the stars for many days, which means that they couldn't navigate or see where they were. After fourteen days of this they were exhausted, hungry and shaken. Then the men on board realized they were approaching land and wanted to let down the small boat and get to shore as quickly as possible. However, Paul says God has told him that no one should jump out of the ship, or they will not survive. The men abandon their plan and stay on board (Acts 27:13–32).

If we think of the ship as representing the gospel of Jesus Christ, then the analogy becomes clear. Things may get rough, and they may be rough for a long time! You might feel like you have to let certain things go that you thought were important. Your ship may become damaged or start to leak. You may be tempted to abandon ship because of the hurtful actions of others, or because some religious leaders don't act like you think they should. Or you may be tempted to jump overboard because so many others around you are leaving their faith. It may look like jumping into the water is a better alternative, but remember Paul and do not leave the ship! Following Jesus Christ is the only way to come safely through the storm.

The truth of the matter is that a person can't prove that God is real any more than a person can prove that He isn't. There isn't scientific proof either way, because that is what faith is. It is trusting, without knowing all the answers. There have been times when I felt I could say, "I know that God is real," and there have been times where all I could muster was, "I'm not sure if God is real or not, but I am choosing to believe He is." We cannot know 100% for sure until we see Him again, but until then, choose to believe that He is real. Choose to believe that Jesus Christ lives. Choose faith and hope, and never abandon ship.

6. LIFE IS JUST TOO HARD. HOW CAN I OVERCOME MY DIFFICULTIES?

One of my favorite things about martial arts is board breaking. It makes you feel so powerful, and it's very satisfying. It has also taught me quite a few things about overcoming challenges.

One of the top questions I'm asked is if breaking a board hurts. It can definitely sting or bruise a bit, but it actually hurts much, much more if you hit the board and don't break it! A lot of people will hesitate and hold back because they're afraid it will hurt. Then, because they don't use their full power, the board doesn't break, and it hurts more than if they had just gone for it 100%. To overcome challenges, you have to commit 100% and let go of your fears!

I also quickly learned that my ability to break the board was either greatly helped or hindered depending on who was holding the board for me. Did you know that if the person holding your board is strong and able to plant their feet, lock out their arms and hold the board tight and steady, it will be much easier to break? On the other hand, if the person holding your board doesn't really know what they're doing or if they are not strong enough, you will have a much harder time breaking the board.

To break through challenges, remember that Jesus Christ is the ultimate board holder! He has perfect knowledge and perfect strength. He is the one holding your troubles and your challenges in his hands, making them easier to break through.

Lastly, when you break a board, you actually want to aim all the way through the board to what's on the other side. If you just focus on aiming at the board itself, your energy and power will stop at the board instead of traveling through it to the other side. When you face challenges, remember to focus on the joy and blessings on the other side of the trial instead of focusing on the difficulty of the problem itself.

7. I'M SO IMPERFECT. I'LL NEVER BE GOOD ENOUGH!

You don't have to be perfect to make a difference. In fact, if you wait to be perfect first, you will never begin. I remember one time when I was really struggling. I have a hard time being patient with myself and my weaknesses, and I was fed up with myself and feeling like I was never going to be the person I wanted to be. I wanted so badly to be perfect! As I was pouring my heart out in prayer one day, the following words came distinctly to my mind:

"You put so much pressure on yourself to be perfect."

The words were not a judgment or condemnation. They felt full of love. I was instantly flooded with a feeling of peace. I think the important word in that phrase was "You." I was the one putting the pressure on myself to be perfect. The Lord does not expect us to be perfect now. He knows it is an eternal process and He does not condemn us for our current weaknesses.

But what about in the meantime? How can we possibly do such great things when we are so flawed and imperfect? The secret to this question is that we don't have to be perfect because the Lord is! He makes up the difference between our desires and our abilities! He invites us to become perfect through Him. Perfection is simply not possible on our own, but through Christ we can do all things.

8. WHY DOES LIFE SEEM TO GET HARDER THE MORE I TRY TO DO GOOD?

It's no secret that you can't fight on both sides of a war at the same time, right? If you declare yourself loyal to one side, you can't also be loyal to the other side. It makes sense that when you decide to fight for one side, the other side automatically becomes your opponent and will actively try to fight against you.

It's the same with the war between good and evil. Once we declare our allegiance to God, we can expect that Satan will be angry and try to attack us. He will do all he can to try and get us to change sides or even to give up the fight completely. Satan knows your power and your abilities, and he will do everything he can to stop you from reaching your potential and fighting against him. In other words, life can be getting harder, not because you are doing things wrong but because you are doing things right!

This knowledge is not to scare or discourage you but to help you be better prepared to face the onslaught. Remember, you are on the Lord's side and it IS the winning side! Light dispels the darkness—always! Follow your leader, Jesus Christ, and He will protect you and help you to withstand the enemy!

ABOUT THE
AUTHOR

Kathryn Lee Moss is an author and speaker, as well as an Emmy-nominated writer and director. She holds a master of arts degree in theatre from the University of London. In 2016 Kathryn created the My World My Time Project to help teach traditional values by bringing to life inspiring stories and heroes from the past.

Kathryn has been invited to share her messages of faith and courage at churches, prisons, schools, and conferences throughout the US and Europe. Her feature film, *Resistance Movement*, and accompanying documentary, *A Time for Resistance*, tell the incredible true story of three teens who had the courage to fight against Hitler.

When she's not trying to change the world, Kathryn can be found in the Taekwondo studio, with a hard-earned, much-loved black belt around her waist. Follow her at www.kathrynleemoss.com.

Scan to visit

www.KathrynLeeMoss.com